HOLDING A MIRROR UP T

Shakespeare has been dubbed the greatest psychologist of all time. This book seeks to prove that statement by comparing the playwright's fictional characters with real-life examples of violent individuals, from criminals to political actors. For Gilligan and Richards, the propensity to kill others, even (or especially) when it results in the killer's own death, is the most serious threat to the continued survival of humanity. In this volume, the authors show how humiliated men, with their desire for retribution and revenge, apocalyptic violence and political religions, justify and commit violence, and how love and restorative justice can prevent violence. Although our destructive power is far greater than anything that existed in his day, Shakespeare has much to teach us about the psychological and cultural roots of all violence. In this book the authors tell what Shakespeare shows, through the stories of his characters: what causes violence and what prevents it.

JAMES GILLIGAN, Professor of Clinical Psychiatry at New York University, wrote *Violence* (1996), *Preventing Violence* (2001), and *Why Some Politicians Are More Dangerous than Others* (2011), a Times Literary Supplement "Book of the Year," and coauthored *The Dangerous Case of Donald Trump* (2016), a *New York Times* best-seller. His advice has been sought by President Clinton, Tony Blair, Kofi Annan, the World Health Organization, and the World Court.

DAVID A. J. RICHARDS is Professor of Law at New York University. He is the author of over twenty books, including *Free Speech and the Politics of Identity* (1999), *Disarming Manhood: Roots of Ethical Resistance* (2005), *The Deepening Darkness: Patriarchy, Resistance, and Democracy's Future* (Cambridge University Press, 2009, with Carol Gilligan), and *Why Love Leads to Justice: Love across the Boundaries* (Cambridge University Press, 2015).

HOLDING A MIRROR UP TO NATURE

Shame, Guilt, and Violence in Shakespeare

JAMES GILLIGAN

New York University

DAVID A. J. RICHARDS

NYU Law School

CAMBRIDGE
UNIVERSITY PRESS

CAMBRIDGE
UNIVERSITY PRESS

University Printing House, Cambridge CB2 8BS, United Kingdom

One Liberty Plaza, 20th Floor, New York, NY 10006, USA

477 Williamstown Road, Port Melbourne, VIC 3207, Australia

314–321, 3rd Floor, Plot 3, Splendor Forum, Jasola District Centre, New Delhi – 110025, India

103 Penang Road, #05–06/07, Visioncrest Commercial, Singapore 238467

Cambridge University Press is part of the University of Cambridge.

It furthers the University's mission by disseminating knowledge in the pursuit of education, learning, and research at the highest international levels of excellence.

www.cambridge.org
Information on this title: www.cambridge.org/9781108833394
DOI: 10.1017/9781108980609

First published 2022

A catalogue record for this publication is available from the British Library.

Library of Congress Cataloging-in-Publication Data
NAMES: Gilligan, James, author. | Richards, David A. J., author.
TITLE: Holding a mirror up to nature : shame, guilt, and violence in Shakespeare / James Gilligan, New York University, David A.J. Richards, NYU Law School.
DESCRIPTION: 1 Edition. | New York, NY : Cambridge University Press, 2021. | Includes bibliographical references and index.
IDENTIFIERS: LCCN 2021025972 (print) | LCCN 2021025973 (ebook) | ISBN 9781108833394 (hardback) | ISBN 9781108970396 (paperback) | ISBN 9781108980609 (epub)
SUBJECTS: LCSH: Murder–Psychological aspects. | Guilt. | Shame. | Violence–Psychological aspects. | Shakespeare, William, 1564-1616–Psychology.
CLASSIFICATION: LCC HV6515 .G47 2021 (print) | LCC HV6515 (ebook) | DDC 364.152/3–dc23
LC record available at https://lccn.loc.gov/2021025972
LC ebook record available at https://lccn.loc.gov/2021025973

ISBN 978-1-108-83339-4 Hardback
ISBN 978-1-108-97039-6 Paperback

For Carol Gilligan and Donald Levy

The poet, as such, does not think thoughts; he makes them; though it may be for us to think the thoughts which he has made. The meanings here discussed are not insisted on by the poetry; they emerge only to a sensitive and listening enquiry. They are rather suggested than said. But that is no reason why we, with due care, should not proceed to say them: it is our business to say them.

—G. Wilson Knight, *The Wheel of Fire: Interpretations of Shakespearean Tragedy* (New York: Meridian, 1947), p. 366

Be not too tame neither, but let your own discretion be your tutor. Suit the action to the word, the word to the action, with this special observance – that you o'erstep not the modest of nature. For anything so o'erdone is from the purpose of playing whose end, both at the first and now, was and is to hold as 'twere the mirror up to Nature to show Virtue her feature, Scorn her own image, and the very age and body of the time his form and pressure.

—William Shakespeare, *Hamlet*, III.ii.16–24

Contents

Introduction

Can We Learn from Shakespeare about the Causes and Prevention of Violence?

When I (James Gilligan) first encountered Walter Manstein, a distinguished-looking man in his late forties, he had just strangled his wife to death with the leash of her pet dog. He came into my orbit because he had been admitted to the prison psychiatric hospital, of which I was the medical director, for a pre-trial psychiatric evaluation. As bizarre as his crime was, it was no more gruesome than the murders that had been committed by many of the other violent men I had seen.

But Walter was a prominent and respected member of society, a successful publisher in one of the largest cities in the state, the father of a daughter, and the husband of a woman to whom he had been married for twenty years, and with whom, as he made clear, he had wanted to remain married – until the night of the murder. When I first met him, I found it almost impossible to understand why in God's name a person whose prior behavior gave every evidence of strong moral character and psychological stability, and who had so many advantages that it would seem he had everything to lose, would end his wife's life, ruin their daughter's life, and effectively end his own life as well.

When I read the police report that accompanied him, the first thing I learned was that immediately after killing his wife, Walter had run out of the house and into his car, which he drove straight into a local reservoir, in an attempt to drown himself – but the car did not completely submerge, and he climbed out of it and lay collapsed on the bank, where the police found and arrested him. He himself could say practically nothing to me except to repeat over and over again that he was "the greatest sinner who had ever lived" and that he expected to be executed by the state, which he felt he deserved. Indeed, he was frustrated by the fact that his attempt to kill himself had failed.

So why had he done something so brutal to his wife, and so irreversibly damaging and destructive to everyone else involved? When he became

I

capable of talking coherently, within the next few days, he revealed that he had committed this murder on the night of their twentieth wedding anniversary. He had hoped that this anniversary would result in a restoration of closeness between himself and his wife, who he felt had become increasingly distant from him over the previous few years. He recalled that he had heard rumors, and others had insinuated to him, that she had attempted to persuade some of the businessmen whose advertisements he needed for the success of his publication to withdraw their support – though he could not understand why she would do this.

However, his hopes for a reconciliation were increasing, as the evening went on, when she handed him a card to celebrate their anniversary. When he opened it, however, what he discovered was that she had crossed out the repeated phrase "Love is" and replaced it with "Love was." While he was still struggling with the implications of that emotional body-blow, she capped it with the remark, "Twenty years, what a waste!" Because he had allowed himself to imagine that she would love him, and to hope for that outcome, he was doubly vulnerable to feelings of shame and humiliation over being so massively rejected: shamed because of what she did, which was to reject him, but also shamed because of what he had done, which was to make himself vulnerable to her and dependent on her by wanting her to love him, and also foolish and naïve enough to expect that she could love him, thus letting himself be deceived and fooled, and made a fool of, by imagining that she might love him, which he now had to admit was merely wishful thinking, and thus foolish on his part. He felt that he had been blind, so out of touch with what her real feelings (or lack of feelings) toward him were, that he had let her deceive and fool him, thus letting her make a fool of him, by showing how foolish he was to think that she could consider him worthy of her love.

When they went to bed that night, he said, he did not merely feel crushed; he said, "I was drowning in an ocean of hate!" He could hardly sleep, and in the middle of the night, only half awake, he impulsively grabbed the leash of the pet dog she loved and strangled her to death with it. But immediately after doing so, he realized what he had done: he had killed the woman he had married and had loved at least enough to want her to love him in return; he could never bring her back to life, she was dead forever; and he had ruined the life of his daughter, who could never recover from the trauma of the fact that her father had murdered her mother. To say merely that he felt guilty would be an understatement: he felt overwhelmingly guilty – "the worst sinner who had ever lived" – and felt the only thing he deserved was death and damnation. It was not he who ran to his car and drove it into the reservoir, to drown himself. It was his guilt feelings that ran him to the car, drove it, and attempted to drown him.

I was very familiar with Freud's notion that aggression is caused by an instinct, but that clearly did not explain this case, or the others I was seeing. For instincts (to eat, to drink, to reproduce) are universal, whereas both murder and suicide are highly selective and relatively rare behaviors.[1] I searched my mind for any way to understand how someone with so much to live for could do something so unthinkable. And then I realized I had just met Othello.

This is a book about the causes and prevention of violence. I (James Gilligan) am a psychiatrist who has specialized in the study of violence, and David Richards is a professor of law who has critiqued the criminal justice system which our society has created in an attempt to solve the problem of violence. To the question, "Why Shakespeare?" in a book about violence, our answer is: because he has more to teach us about the proclivity of humans to kill others and themselves than any other author we know of. When we draw on clinical evidence (observations of and quotations from murderers, rapists, and others incarcerated in prisons or prison psychiatric hospitals in the United States or other countries), we are drawing on my (James Gilligan's) experience. In our interpretation of the plays, we draw on David Richards' decades of studies of retributive justice, as well as his analysis of patriarchy and its effects on men. We also draw on our collaborative work teaching together at New York University's School of Law (where we use Shakespeare's plays as dramatizations of retributive vs. restorative justice), and our discussions outside class, as well as, historically, my study of Shakespeare with Professor Harry Levin at Harvard College.

I found that Shakespeare proved to be the most valuable resource for understanding violence when I was chosen to lead a team of mental health

---

[1] Even in America, which has the highest murder rates in the world among developed nations, there are usually no more than five to ten homicides per year among every 100,000 people, and only nine to fifteen suicides. Hardly consistent with the notion of a universal, spontaneously occurring instinctual behavior! Even among the "lower" animals, any species in which every member was compelled by its instincts to kill every other member of its own species would quickly become extinct. So, contra Freud, it is not "instinct" that causes violence toward one's own species, and most "civilizations" do not prevent or minimize it. On the contrary, as we will show below, violence is caused by the inhibition and frustration of our natural, healthy instincts to form attachments to each other (we are, after all, "social" animals), to love, reproduce, and care for and cooperate with each other and our offspring; and our various cultures and civilizations, far from uniformly inhibiting violent behavior, are, from the standpoint of epidemiology and public health, the main causes of whatever violence does occur – though the degree to which they do this is highly variable, as we discuss below.

professionals in providing psychiatric services for the inmates of the Massachusetts prisons and prison psychiatric hospital in the late 1970s, in order to reduce the level of violence among the inmates of the prison psychiatric hospital for the "criminally insane" (those who were violent because of mental illness) and for the much larger group in the ordinary prisons, each of whose minds was defined by the law not as ill, but as evil (a *mens rea*).

The book itself, the turn to Shakespeare as a source of insight about violence, was born from these experiences, including the encounter with Walter Manstein.

These experiences began when I was chosen by state and federal courts in Boston, the Massachusetts Department of Correction, and the Harvard Medical School to create and direct an innovative program of mental health services on a scale that had not previously existed, for a prison system that was in the midst of a war zone–level epidemic of violence – homicides, suicides, riots, hostage-taking, gang rapes, arson, and other acts of violence – that had led to the deaths of hundreds of prisoners, guards, visitors, and staff members throughout the entire decade of the 1970s. The courts concluded that most of this violence was caused by severe but undiagnosed and untreated or inadequately treated psychopathology among the prisoners (and some of the guards), some of which preexisted their incarceration, but much of which appeared to be caused or exacerbated by the conditions within the prisons. And since the criminal justice system had proven itself incapable of ending this epidemic (and in fact was one of the major causes of it), the court turned to the mental health system.

However, while the mental health system had long considered one form of violence, suicide, a mental health problem, it had relegated violence against other people, such as murder, to the criminal justice system, and thus largely ignored it. The criminal justice system, for its part, has ignored the question of what causes violence and how it could be prevented, and restricted itself to judging how evil a particular defendant was and how much punishment they deserve: not what caused their violence, nor what we as a society could do to decrease the frequency with which this kind of behavior occurs in the first place. Even criminology was of little help here, for it restricts itself to the study of crime. Yet most of the violence that is committed is not criminal, and most crimes are not violent: far more people are killed by forms of violence that the legal system either ignores or commands, such as suicide, capital punishment, and participation in wars; and most crimes are not violent, they are property crimes, ingestion of chemical substances whose use has been defined as a crime, or acts committed contrary to "public morals" laws such as those prohibiting gambling or prostitution. So the attempt to discover the causes and prevention of violence actually got little help from either the mental health system, the criminal justice system, or the academic discipline called criminology.

Faced with this paucity of previous research into the problem of violence, I found that I could only begin to make sense of the violence that I saw by way of mythic and tragic literature – the Bible, the Greek and Roman classics, and Shakespeare. That literature was, and still is, the most adequate representation of the human experience of violent behavior, or at least more faithful to what my own experience of working with violent people showed me, than anything I found in the contemporary literature in psychiatry, psychoanalysis, psychology, criminal law, or criminology.

It was not simply that only the Greek tragedies and those of Shakespeare, only the horrors described in Thucydides and the Bible, map with fidelity the universe of human violence as I witnessed it, without euphemism or bowdlerization, without minimizing the facts or intellectualizing their horror. It was only through thinking in terms of that literature that I found a way to mediate between ordinary sanity and humanity, on the one hand, and unimaginable horror and monstrosity, on the other. Compared with the tragedies that I saw and heard of daily in the worlds in which I was working, the abstractions of the social sciences – including even the one best equipped theoretically to deal with those tragedies, psychoanalysis – were pale imitations of reality, like the shadows on Plato's cave.

In the worlds I worked in, Oedipus was not a theory, not a "complex." I met Oedipus, met him twice – two men who had killed their fathers and then blinded themselves, not on the stage, not in a textbook, but in real life. One by banging his head against the wall of his cell until he had damaged his occipital lobe, the visual center of his brain, and the other by staring at the sun: yet while their methods differed, both wound up just as blind as Oedipus.

I met Medea – a woman who killed her children in response to her husband's infatuation with another woman.

I met Othello, as I mentioned above, and I met him again, when a college professor who had murdered his wife felt so guilty that he did succeed in killing himself, even after having been placed on maximum suicide precautions ("constant observation").

I met Richard III: a man who felt that his disfiguring deformity prevented him from being loved by any woman, and who therefore decided to revenge himself on the world by killing two people and attempting to kill many others.

I met Edmund, Gloucester's bastard son in *King Lear* who arranges to have his father's eyes gouged out, and the sons of Tamora in *Titus Andronicus*, who cut out the tongue of Titus's daughter Lavinia, when I saw a young man who committed these same grotesque mutilations on a woman he killed when he thought he appeared inferior and inadequate in her eyes and those of his other peers, as well as insulted and taunted by their tongues.

I met Samson (the archetypal "son of Sam"), and Shakespeare's version of the same pattern of motivation and intent, in *Timon of Athens*, and met him many times – men who felt so overwhelmingly and irreversibly shamed and humiliated and defeated that they did not know how to bring their emotional pain to an end except by destroying the entire world, killing everyone – the audience observing their shame – and ending their own lives as well, bringing the roof down on everyone's head. As one prisoner put it, "I am at war against the whole world" – words that could have come from Timon's own mouth.

These experiences led me to think that these myths and tragedies must have originated not as products of fantasy – as the symbolic, "conscious" representation of fantasies that are unconscious in the minds of normal people, as Freud said about *Oedipus Tyrannus* – but rather as attempts to describe and represent, to cope with and make sense of, indeed to survive, emotionally and mentally, the *actual* crimes and atrocities that people have inflicted on each other and themselves for as far back into history as our collective memories extend. And have continued to do in the present, somewhere in the world, every single day.

"In the beginning was the deed," as Goethe put it in *Faust*; and he may have been right, the act may have preceded the word and the thought. It still does, in the violent people that I saw. Much of the therapy with these men, for they were mostly men, consisted of facilitating their ability to talk and think about their grievances, their fears, and their rage, rather than expressing them in acts of violence. Ways to accomplish this included having them witness performances of Shakespeare's plays or perform those plays themselves, in the United States and England,[2] in which they were astonished to see characters in those plays committing the same acts of violence that they had, or having them write plays themselves, about an

---

[2] Murray Cox, ed., *Shakespeare Comes to Broadmoor: "The Actors Come Hither"* (London: Jessica Kingsley, 1992).

experience in their own lives that had turned them toward a life of violence. For the only alternative to violence, as my colleagues and I along with these men discovered, is words – just as for these violent men, the only alternative to words had been violence.

What I observed in the prisons – and what Shakespeare shows us in his plays – is that violence is itself a kind of proto-language, whose purpose is to communicate an emotional and moral message by means of symbolic actions on the ground; at least for them, "actions speak louder than words." They used violent actions not just as a substitute for thoughts and beliefs but as a way of acting them out, expressing them in action, and as a way to stop feeling the painful emotions of shame and humiliation.

Shame and its opposite, pride and honor, are among the words most often used by Shakespeare to describe the motivations for violence in his characters. And he shows characters resorting to the most extreme and grotesque forms of violence and mutilation, such as cutting out the eyes and tongues of their victims, in an effort to avoid or eliminate the feeling of being shamed. These gruesome acts serve the emotional purpose, in the language of magical thinking, of protecting the perpetrator from being shamed; for as Aristotle said, more than two millennia ago, "shame dwells in the eyes" (of others), and is inflicted by their tongues, in the form of insults, slights, and slanders. Shakespeare also mentioned repeatedly how his violent characters felt shamed in the eyes of others, and by their tongues. But what Shakespeare did, which the violent men I saw in the prisons had not been able to do when they committed their acts of violence, was to put into words what the psychological and moral meaning of their actions was (to them) and why they had committed these atrocities.

I was able to use the prisons as the equivalent of a social-psychological research laboratory in which to learn about the causes and prevention of violence, wherever it occurred and on whatever scale, from homicide and suicide to war and genocide, just as a microbiology laboratory, in identifying the causes of individual illnesses, also discovers what causes epidemics and pandemics of those same causes of death outside the world of the laboratory – and to test the generalizability of those discoveries to pandemics of collective political violence on a worldwide scale, in work I engaged in with the World Health Organization's Department of Injuries and Violence Prevention, the World Court in the Hague, and the World Economic Forum's Committee on Negotiations and Conflict Resolution.

In doing this work, to paraphrase *Richard II*, I was "studying how I may compare this prison where I [work] unto the world" (V.v.1–2). Indeed, many scholars, in law, political science, and sociology have recognized how much prisons serve as a microcosm of the social macrocosm in which they exist. As Dostoevsky put it, "The degree of civilization in a society can be judged by entering its prisons."[3]

To understand violence it is necessary to recognize and understand what grievances motivate violence, and how they determine whom the violence is directed toward. It is also necessary to understand the different cultures in which violent acts take place, and how they co-determine the extent and direction of the violence that occurs.

For helping us to climb those mountains, Shakespeare is an invaluable guide. In play after play, he shows us exactly what motivates violence, whether in the context of intimate interpersonal relations or of wars between nations, and what we need to do if we want to prevent it. But he shows us this in the form of a story, a narrative of the life history and the moment-to-moment thoughts and feelings of the persons committing the violence – not as an abstract theory. What we are setting out to do in this book, then, is to tell, in the form of theory, what Shakespeare has shown us, and shown us very clearly, in the form of plays, dramas that bring to life on the stage the thoughts and feelings of people who act violently, and the cultural contexts in which they do so – or refrain from doing so.

It was Freud himself early in his development of psychoanalysis who worried about how different his method was from what was generally taken to be science – or, if you prefer, from the view of science that he previously had held:

> Like other neuropathologists I was trained to employ local diagnoses and electro-prognosis, and it still strikes me myself as strange that the case histories I write should read like short stories and that, as one might say, they lack the serious stamp of science. I must console myself with the reflection that the nature of the subject is evidently responsible for this, rather than any preference of my own.[4]

"The nature of the subject," as Freud puts it, is human psychology. It is for this reason that Freud came to explore literary narratives (including Shakespeare and the ancient Greek myths and tragedies, from Oedipus to Narcissus) in his work, and to recognize in his use of literature the everyday fact that is part of everyone's experience, that we can only begin to understand any of our fellow humans, or even ourselves, when we

---

[3] As quoted in a Supreme Court decision by Justice Anthony Kennedy.   [4] Freud (1973), p. 160.

become acquainted with the story of a person's life – their personal life history – which constitutes a narrative, a plot.

The Greek term for stories or narratives is *mythos*, the root of "myth" – which is why myths, and the literary works that incorporate and elaborate myths, are invaluable sources of information about the universal, archetypal, and constantly repeated patterns of human lives – people's experiences, their thoughts and feelings about those experiences, and the behaviors they engage in in response to them.

Freud and many later psychoanalysts have pointed out how much the healing power of psychoanalysis comes from its ability to enable people to construct and reconstruct the story, or narrative, of their own lives, and to see how their life histories are not just "one damned thing after another" (as Henry Ford said world history was), a tissue of randomness and chaos, but rather a comprehensible and intelligible sequence of events related to each other in terms of cause and effect (as Thucydides said world history was).[5] That is, to paraphrase Shakespeare, there is always a method – an intelligible structure – even in what may appear to be utter madness.

That is precisely why Shakespeare's plays are so valuable. They are one of the richest sources of insights about human nature and human psychology. For just as Freud's case histories read like short stories, or fictions, Shakespeare's plays (his fictions) can be read as case histories. And just as Freud understood his case histories as if they were short stories, and derived his theories from them, we will attempt to understand Shakespeare's plays as if they were case histories, and derive our theories from them – while also showing how our own case histories of violent people can be understood by grasping what Shakespeare has shown us in his "case histories."

Despite all the changes in history and culture, there are certain constants in human nature, and Shakespeare, as usual, is a profound observer. As he put it,

> There is a history in all men's lives,
> Figuring the natures of the times deceas'd
> The which observ'd, a man may prophesy,
> With a near aim, of the main chance

---

[5] That is why R. G. Collingwood (1994), pp. 29–30, called Thucydides not "the father of history"– that was Herodotus – but rather "the father of psychological history," meaning that he was attempting not just to record particular events but to discover what general principles, or "psychological laws," they illustrated and were caused by. The same could be said of Shakespeare's "history plays," which are not records of historical facts as much as they are illustrations of general psychological principles that are among the determinants of political history. See, for example, Greenblatt (2018).

As yet not come to life, who in their seeds
And weak beginning lie intreasured.
Such things become the hatch and brood of time,
And by the necessary form of this
King Richard might create a perfect guess
That great Northumberland, then false to him,
Would of that seed grow greater falseness . . .

To which King Henry IV replies, "Are these things then necessities? Then let us meet them like necessities" (*2 Henry IV*, III.ii.80–94).

As these quotations convey, Shakespeare, writing at the dawn of the scientific revolution that reconstructed the way people think (when they are thinking scientifically), incorporated into his plays the replacement of the mythological and theological concepts in terms of which people had previously interpreted their experience – namely, as the product of "fate" or "providence" or "destiny," over which, by definition, they had little or no control – by the scientific notion of determinism (cause and effect). Before Shakespeare made psychological ways of thinking possible, and illustrated them in his plays, much of life had been experienced as an inexplicable and uncontrollable matter of good or bad luck – or the "will of God."

In ancient Greece, which invented the precursors of modern science and of tragic drama that were most influential to the men who led the transition from the medieval to the modern world view in western Europe in the seventeenth century, Heraclitus saw how to advance from myth to psychological science when he reconstructed the concept of fate (or the will of the gods), about which neither knowledge nor control is possible, into the formula that it is a man's character that determines his fate. According to Heraclitus, our habitual behavior patterns, and the motives that cause them (called our character) are among the major determinants not only of the events that happen to us but, even more importantly, of how we respond to them.

Yet Shakespeare shows us that these variables work in both directions: for in the speech just quoted he acknowledges how much a man's fate (what we call today his biological inheritance – for example, in an earlier play, Richard III's hunchback – and the social environment into which he was born) also determines his character, and that it is the interaction between the two – his character and his life experiences – during the course of his life history, that determines his behavior, which can be understood and predicted the more we (and he) know about his life history.

What is remarkably modern, however, is Shakespeare's assumption in this same speech of the basis of modern science (from physics to psychology), namely, of determinism, or necessity. This is what enables us both to explain and to understand our past behavior, as a matter of cause and effect, and to predict (and potentially change) the behavior we will engage in in the future. As Shakespeare's contemporary Francis Bacon recognized, knowledge is power. And self-knowledge increases one's power over oneself, one's life, and one's society.

The classics scholar Werner Jaeger has described the ancient Greek tragedian Euripides as "the first psychologist."[6] We suggest that Shakespeare, among the first and certainly the greatest of modern tragedians, is the first psychologist of the modern era. Because he is so much closer to us, both in time and in culture, we focus our book on what we can learn from him about human psychology in our own time.

Shakespeare wrote stories, not theories; he provided the raw material – you might say, the empirical data – from which we can derive the theories that we will need, if we are ever going to become able to understand the aspect of human psychology and behavior called violence. What we will do in this book is a form of show and tell, where Shakespeare shows, and we tell what he shows, about the causes and prevention of violence. We will offer theories that have been tested against the actual case histories of violent patients, as well as by quantitative and statistical data, such as measures of fluctuations in the rates of homicide and suicide under differing psychological and social conditions.

We begin, then, by saying that Shakespeare's plays repeatedly demonstrate and illuminate the sequence of psychological and sociocultural events that culminate in, or cause, violent behavior: namely, an actual or threatened loss of love, which causes shame, which hate, which causes violence. Loss of love → shame → hate → violence.

It is no accident that shame has many names, one of which is ridicule (being mocked or laughed at). And the most direct and immediate way to stop people from ridiculing or laughing at you is to make them weep instead, which can be done most definitively by subjecting them to violence. Shakespeare illuminates this brilliantly in the scene from *Henry V* where the French Dauphin mocks or ridicules Henry by sending him a gift, not of royal treasure but of tennis balls. Henry responds:

> ... tell the pleasant prince this mock of his
> Hath turned his balls to gun-stones, and his soul
> Shall stand sore charged for the wasteful vengeance

---

[6] Jaeger (1965), p. 353.

That shall fly with them; for many a thousand widows
Shall this his mock mock out of their dear husbands;
Mock mothers from their sons, mock castles down;
And some are yet ungotten and unborn
That shall have cause to curse the Dolphin's scorn.
. . . And tell the Dauphin
His jest will savor but of shallow wit
When thousands weep more than did laugh at it.

(I.ii.281–96)

It is true that creating, achieving, or producing things that are valued by
other people can command respect and lead to honors, prestige, status,
wealth, power, and sources of pride, self-esteem, and esteem from others,
and that this can be an equally effective and even more permanent source
of honor than destructive or antisocial behavior. The experience of com-
peting successfully in nonviolent pursuits and attaining a level of achievement high enough to reach one's level of ambition or aspiration can heal
the narcissistic wounds that constitute shame. However, achievement and
creativity require time, patience, talent, education, and labor, and many
people and peoples have not had or have not perceived themselves as
having access to those internal and external resources, whereas violence
always lies ready to hand (literally).

That this fear, the fear of shame, humiliation, and ridicule, can be one
of the most powerful motives for individual and collective violence is well
attested to throughout history. At the very dawn of Western history, in our
oldest surviving epic, the *Iliad*, the first recorded war is attributed to the
shame that Menelaus felt when a Trojan prince, Paris, dishonored him by
running off with his wife, Helen. The very fact that both sides – Greeks
and Trojans – were willing to commit whole armies and the entire
population of a large city to total destruction over this question of honor
is the most powerful argument against trivializing, oversimplifying, or
underestimating the power, complexity, and dangerousness of the feelings
of shame and humiliation; for it is hard to reach any other conclusion than
that both the Achaeans (the Greeks) and the Trojans literally preferred
death – in fact, mass slaughter, of themselves as well as of their enemies –
to "dishonor."

Equally compelling examples of wars or terrorist attacks resulting from
the wish to undo shame and restore national honor, no matter the cost in
death and suffering, recur throughout history, culminating most appall-
ingly in the last century when Hitler came to power on the campaign
promise to "undo the shame of Versailles." In the United States, Presidents

Johnson and Nixon continued the war in Vietnam for years in order to avoid "losing face" by becoming the first American president to lose a war. And in the twenty-first century, Osama bin Laden explained that the motive for the suicide bombings of 9/11 was to get revenge: "What America is tasting now is only a copy of what we have tasted. Our Islamic nation has been tasting the same for more than 80 years, of humiliation and contempt" to which "the entire Islamic nation" had been subjected by the Western powers, of which the United States became the symbol.[7]

A famous illustration of the role of shame in causing murder and of guilt in preventing it can be seen in *Macbeth*. Lady Macbeth engages in a relentless campaign to shame her husband into murdering the reigning king, Duncan, so that he will become the king and she the queen. She sets out explicitly to diminish any feelings of guilt or conscience that might stand in his way, ruminating that

> I fear thy nature,
> It is too full o' the milk of human kindness
> To catch the nearest way. Thou wouldst be great,
> Art not without ambition, but without
> The illness should attend it.

She thereupon resolves to cause in him that "illness" – that is, to inflate his ambition to murderous dimensions by shaming his manhood, saying that were he not willing to commit murder he would be not a man but a woman (which, in a patriarchal culture, would be the ultimate shame).

Many psychoanalysts, such as Ernest Jones and Otto Fenichel, have noted that ambition is specifically stimulated by shame. As Fenichel put it, "the aim of ambition ... is to prove that there is no need to be ashamed anymore." And he also noticed that "the 'success' which is the goal of the ambition may acquire the ... meaning of killing ... and therefore," in those who are capable of guilt feelings, "become prohibited."[8] Lady Macbeth anticipated both of those discoveries by centuries. When Macbeth hesitates to kill the king, she taunts him by questioning whether he has the courage to realize his ambition: "Wouldst thou have that Which thou esteem'st the ornament of life, And live a coward in thine own esteem, letting 'I dare not' wait upon 'I would'?" (I.vii.41–3). Following

---

[7] From the first public comment by Osama bin Laden following 9/11/2001, from a videotaped statement broadcast on October 7, 2001, by Al Jazeera in Qatar, as translated from the Arabic by Reuters, and published in the *New York Times*, October 8, 2001.

[8] Fenichel (1945), pp. 139 and 493.

his first murder, when Macbeth begins to show compunctions, or guilt feelings, about what he has done, she shames him with the taunting comment, "My hands are of your color [red, bloody]; but I shame To wear a heart so white" (II.ii.61–2). Later, when Macbeth hallucinates Banquo's ghost after having arranged for his murder, Lady Macbeth shames him again by directly questioning his adequacy as a man:

> Are you a man?
> . . . these flaws and starts . . . would well become
> A woman's story at a winter's fire,
> Authorized by her grandam. Shame itself,
> Why do you make such faces?
> . . . What? quite unmann'd in folly?
> . . . Fie, for shame!"
>
> (III.iv.55–73)

Turning now to guilt: guilt is both the opposite and the antagonist of shame. The capacity to feel guilt signifies the presence of what we call a conscience. It is based not on a feeling of weakness and a fear of humiliation, defeat, or weakness, as shame is, but rather on the fear that one possesses so much power that one could injure the people by whom one has felt shamed, and thus angered, but toward whom one also feels love, empathy, or responsibility.

Shame consists of an absence or deficiency of pride or self-love, so that to the extent that one feels shamed one cannot emotionally afford to love others: one has to hoard whatever love is available for oneself. Shame is the emotion people are vulnerable to when they feel they are too weak, incompetent, and unskilled, too inadequate, to meet the challenges they face at each new stage of development, from infancy to old age. Under favorable circumstances, they are able to develop whatever new strengths and skills are needed, and to replace shame with pride. And when they achieve pride, or self-love, they can emotionally afford to love others as well.

Love is the emotion that generates the wish to help the people one loves, and even to protect them, rather than harm them. But when people are capable of loving others, they become prone to feelings of guilt when they become angry at those they love, or experience impulses to harm them. Thus feelings of pride are the necessary prerequisite for, and companion of, the capacity to feel guilt: without the feeling of pride, there can be no feeling of guilt; but where there is both pride, or self-love, and ambivalence (the coexistence of love and hate toward others), there will be guilt. That is why pride is considered the deadliest of the "Seven Deadly Sins," in the guilt-ethic of Christianity: pride and guilt are, so to speak, joined at the hip. But by the same token, feelings of shame are accompanied by feelings of innocence, for if you feel you are too weak and unskilled to harm anyone, you cannot be guilty – but they can hurt you. Thus shame tends to motivate conspiracy theories, or delusions of persecution, that others wish to harm you.

In saying this, we have to underscore that the psychology we elaborate here whereby loss of love leads to shame and shame to hate, which in turn leads to violence, is primarily a psychology of men (in what we will describe in Chapter 1 as patriarchal shame cultures). For according to what can be called the "rules of patriarchy," violence by men can serve to undo or prevent shame and restore or establish honor. For women in such cultures, the opposite is true: violent behavior on their part, in response to whatever feelings of shame they experience, is more likely to provoke further shaming, rather than to elicit the opposite, respect and honor. Thus neither Lady Macbeth nor Volumnia can gain honor through being violent themselves. They can gain honor only vicariously, through the men they are attached to – their husband or son, respectively – by shaming him into being violent for them.

The two of us, James Gilligan and David Richards, as well as Carol Gilligan, who has also cowritten with David, have focused extensively on the different ways in which patriarchy deforms the characters of men and women, affecting specifically their capacity to love.[9] To put it succinctly, patriarchal cultures shame men if they are unwilling to protect their honor by means of violence, whereas patriarchal cultures shame women, as Virginia Woolf noted, mainly for their sexual activity, most notably for having sex outside marriage.[10] In patriarchy, men are shamed if they refuse to play the role of the patriarch and be dominant and violent, in which case they are called cowards, slaves, boys, women, or (after Shakespeare's time) homosexuals, as we will see with Henry VI, Macbeth, and others; whereas women are shamed for being sexually active (in which case they are called whores or sluts), as well as, for being violent or even aggressive and ambitious in nonviolent ways, bitches.

---

[9] J. Gilligan (1997); J. Gilligan (2002); J. Gilligan (2009); C. Gilligan and Richards (2009); C. Gilligan and Richards (2018).

[10] Woolf (1938), p. 182: "External observation would suggest that a man still feels it a peculiar insult to be taunted with cowardice by a woman in much the same way that a woman feels it a peculiar insult to be taunted with unchastity by a man."

Freud commented once that no one feels guiltier than the saints.[11] That is why they are saints: they would feel too guilty to hurt a butterfly. Working with a population that Freud never had any experience with, I (James Gilligan), discovered that no one feels more innocent than the criminals – no matter how "guilty" they are in the eyes of the law, or of the guilt-ethic that says, "Thou shalt not kill." In fact, the more horrendous the crime, the more innocent they feel. That is not just why they became criminals; it is why they had the emotional capacity, or potentiality, to commit the kinds of acts that we call criminal – for they have not developed the capacity for, and the sensitivity to, feelings of guilt, one of the emotions that inhibit people from harming others. As my colleagues and I used to say, "You rarely meet a guilty man in prison." This does not mean that they would deny that they had committed the act for which they were sentenced to prison. It means that they felt morally justified, and therefore morally innocent, for committing the act: "The bitch deserved it," or "the son of a bitch deserved it."

There were exceptions to these generalizations, though they were rare, such as the two "Othellos" described above – the publisher and the college professor who killed their wives and then attempted or succeeded in killing themselves. Shakespeare shows how guilt can lead to violence – but when it does, the violence is almost always directed toward the self rather than toward others. For example, Othello kills himself after being overwhelmed by feelings of guilt for having killed Desdemona; Enobarbus kills himself after feeling overcome by guilt for having betrayed Marc Antony; Lady Macbeth loses her will to live and kills herself when she realizes how shaming her husband into committing murder has instigated endless, unlimited bloodshed, more than even she could tolerate. However, guilt does not solve the problem of violence. While it inhibits violence toward others, it merely redirects it onto the self.

Finally, we will suggest that Shakespeare shows how violence can be prevented by transcending the moral emotions of both shame and guilt along with the moral value systems they engender, which we call shame ethics and guilt ethics. In a number of plays, he demonstrates how the transcendence of violence hinges on the capacity to love and, more specifically, the ability to love both self and others. Duke Vincentio in *Measure for Measure*, Polixenes in *The Winter's Tale*, and Prospero in

---

[11] Freud (1961), pp. 125–6: "the more virtuous a man is, the more severe and distrustful is [the super-ego's] behavior, so that ultimately it is precisely those people who have carried saintliness furthest who reproach themselves with the worst sinfulness."

The Tempest all respond, by the end of those plays, to the real, threatened, or suspected violence of others not by moralistic, retaliatory violence of their own (revenge, or that euphemism for revenge, punishment, or "retributive justice") but rather by giving the real or putative offenders an example of behavior that is nonpunitive and nonviolent – a response that exemplifies and fosters loving behavior instead, whether in weddings and marriages or in the renewal of interrupted friendships or marriages, leading to forgiveness, love, and reconciliation among everyone involved, with which all of those plays end.

In summary, we not only have come to see Shakespeare as the first psychologist in the modern world. We would even claim that his psychological insights into the causes and prevention of violence have never been surpassed by any of his successors. Shakespeare shows what in this book we want to tell. We will begin in Chapter 1 by summarizing the theory of shame and guilt so clearly illuminated by Shakespeare's plays. Following that, we will discuss several of the plays individually, and the various ways in which they can lead us to understand the causes and the prevention of violence.

One of the most important topics we address in this book is Shakespeare's demonstration in *Hamlet* of the problem of moral nihilism, as it has become arguably the main problem of modernity, and of the new forms of individual and collective violence that have come into existence only because of modernity. When Hamlet says that "there is nothing either good or bad but thinking makes it so," he is articulating the discovery of the subjectivity, and hence the arbitrariness, from a cognitive point of view, of moral value judgments, which entails the loss of their credibility and authority. He is paralyzed by his inability to overcome doubts as to his ability to know what he should do. Hamlet thus embodies and represents the need for a new way of thinking (which Shakespeare himself pioneered in his plays), and the discovery of the conditions that facilitate or inhibit our capacity for the most ancient of emotions, love (of self and others). Taken as a whole, Shakespeare's plays bring to life on the stage a problem that we in the world of modernity are still struggling with, while at the same time showing us both the emotional solution (love) and the cognitive solution (psychological understanding, rather than moral condemnation, punishment, and violence). In this respect Shakespeare becomes our contemporary.

CHAPTER I

Shame and Guilt in Personality and Culture

To understand the psychology Shakespeare shows us in his plays, we begin with a brief overview of the opposite and antagonistic moral emotions, shame and guilt, and their role in stimulating or inhibiting violence, from homicide and suicide to war and genocide. We include a discussion, also relevant to Shakespeare's plays, of the moral value systems motivated by shame and guilt (shame ethics vs. guilt ethics), shame-driven versus guilt-ridden character structures, shame cultures versus guilt cultures, and the role of shame and guilt in law (retributive vs. restorative justice) and politics (authoritarian, right-wing tyrannies vs. egalitarian, left-wing democracies). All in preparation for our telling of what Shakespeare shows us through the words and actions of his characters.

The emotions of shame and guilt (and their opposites, pride and innocence, respectively) are as central to human motivation and behavior as love and hate are – because they are love and hate, except as directed toward the self, rather than toward others. Shame is the absence or deficiency of self-love and love from others, and its opposite is pride, or self-love, self-esteem, self-respect, and the feeling of self-worth, as well as love from others, as in being respected, esteemed, and honored by them. The feeling of guilt, or sinfulness, is the presence of self-hate and the feeling of deserving punishment and needing to perform acts of penance; its opposite is the feeling of innocence, the absence of self-hate and self-blame.

We speak of shame as a generic term for a family of related emotions, just as we use the term "flower" to refer to roses, daffodils, and many other species that belong to the same family. The centrality of shame in human emotional life is indicated by its many synonyms: feeling inferior, inadequate, weak, incompetent, ignorant, unlovable, a failure, a loser and so on. Since shame as a feeling always presumes an audience, real or imagined, in whose eyes one feels shamed, shame also includes the feeling of being disrespected by others, humiliated, insulted, dishonored, disgraced, slighted, rejected, unloved, ridiculed, mocked or laughed at by them, or perceived as weak and inferior, and suffering what some Asian cultures call "loss of face," psychoanalysts call "narcissistic injuries," and Alfred Adler called an "inferiority complex." The feelings of envy and jealousy are members of this same family of feelings: one feels inferior to others with respect to whatever one feels jealous or envious about.

Pride or self-love (the opposite of shame) refers to feelings of self-esteem, self-respect, and self-worth, and to receiving or at least deserving love and esteem from others, as in having them respect one's dignity, honor, and reputation.

Guilt and remorse are the feelings of being sinful, culpable, or blame-worthy. Its opposite, the feeling of innocence, is the absence of self-condemnation and self-hate, and the feeling of righteousness, which at the extreme becomes the feeling called self-righteousness.

Shame, because it is the lack of love for the self, motivates directing love toward the self and directing hate, the opposite and extinguisher of love, toward others.

As Freud observed and as everyone who has ever loved knows, we are never as vulnerable as when we love – vulnerable to grief and sadness if someone we love dies, or to shame and humiliation if someone we love does not love us or loves someone else instead. In response to this loss, we may simply choose to defend ourselves against our pain, by withdrawing our love and ceasing to care. Thus we can treat others with indifference, neglect, contempt, and abandonment. Or we may choose an active defense (which is a more powerful weapon against shame), namely, hate, aggression, and violence toward them. Indifference and neglect, however, which is also called passive aggressiveness, can be just as deadly as the active form, overt violence – as, for example, parental neglect of children, neglect of the poor by the rich, and so on.

Thus we can understand hate, whether passive or active, as a defense against the emotional pain of losing love, by reversing our love for the other person or group into hate. In this conception, then, hate and violence are not instincts but rather defenses or protections against an instinct – the normal and healthy instinct to love others – when that exposes us to emotional pain.

To say it differently, shame (the actual or threatened deprivation of love) leads people to want to receive love from others but to give love only to themselves, not to others – just as starving persons may hoard any scraps of food for themselves. Shame also motivates people to direct hate away from themselves and toward others – in fact, to hate others, even to the point of killing them, in order to avoid or undo being shamed by them, and to achieve pride and honor instead. This they can do by demonstrating strength rather than weakness, and transferring shame from themselves onto their victim, which violence does, by proving that their victim is weaker than they are. In *Macbeth*, Shakespeare shows us how a noble soldier comes to kill his king in order to avoid being shamed by his wife for not having the courage (being too cowardly) to do the deed that would raise him in her esteem and enable him to attain the pride and honor of becoming the king himself. In *King Lear*, the children of Lear and Gloucester, who feel themselves less loved by their fathers than their siblings, engage in violence toward their fathers (and siblings) to gain the pride and honor (in the form of wealth, power, and status) they feel deprived of.

Shame and guilt can be considered as dynamic opposites in that shame motivates people to direct hate toward others and love toward themselves, and guilt motivates people to direct hate toward themselves and love toward others.

From a developmental point of view, shame is the precursor and precondition for guilt. This is true on every time scale, such as the moment-to-moment movement from one emotion to the other, as with Othello, who feels shamed when he believes that his wife, Desdemona, has been unfaithful, and then feels guilt when he learns, after having killed her, that, in fact, she had been innocent of that offense and had continued to love him faithfully. Shame also precedes guilt on the larger scale of the human life cycle as people move from one stage of development to another, avoiding shame and achieving pride by mastering the skills and competencies required by each new stage of development. The capacity for feelings of guilt occurs when one realizes that one has achieved so much of those skills and competencies that one possesses the power and ability to injure or kill others (toward whom one has some feelings of love, as well as of hate). And this progression occurs on the much larger time scale of the evolution of whole cultures as they evolve from shame cultures into guilt cultures (or, potentially, beyond either of those categories, as we will discuss below).

To explicate this sequence: shame stimulates hate and thus violent impulses toward others. These impulses in turn stimulate the feeling of guilt, which motivates people to inhibit their hate and violence toward others by redirecting those feelings and impulses toward themselves instead. So, no one feels guilt without first having felt ashamed. For shame is what causes the hate and the violent impulses that guilt redirects toward the self.

To underscore this point, which we will see dramatized in Shakespeare's plays, violent impulses are not the result of an instinct, if by "instinct" we mean what Freud and Konrad Lorenz meant:[1] a universal, inborn impulse or drive to kill others or oneself that is "natural," meaning it occurs spontaneously and universally – and will only grow in strength until it is satisfied by being acted out in the form of violence, as hunger and thirst do until they are satisfied by food and liquids. Likewise, the instinct to reproduce is inborn and occurs spontaneously in all cultural and demographic groups (by definition since any group in which it did not occur would become extinct within one generation).

The desire to socialize, to seek out relationships with other people and form attachments to them, meaning love, is universal among all healthy human beings, as a result of evolution, for it supports life and survival; and when it is absent or deficient, as among those who suffer from autism or personality disorders, the absence itself may endanger life and survival. Thus Aristotle was right when he observed that only gods and beasts can live independently, in isolation from others of their kind, whereas humans are inherently and universally social animals (*zoon politikon*) or political animals (the two adjectives are synonymous). Thus our need and desire for relationships – familial love, friendships, partnerships – appear to be instinctual.

Neither homicide nor suicide, neither war nor capital punishment nor terrorism, occur universally, among all humans. While the potential for violence may be universal – if there were not such a potential, there could never be actual violence – the frequency of actual violence varies enormously from one culture or nation to another at any given time, from one historical epoch to another even within the same national or ethnic group, from one individual to another, and even at different times within the same individual. Eating, drinking, and the desire for sexual as well as non-sexual loving relationships with other humans may be biologically determined and universally experienced instinctual drives (except among rare and damaged individuals), but violence is not. Our potential for violence becomes actualized only when a violent response is provoked by the kind of psycho-social stimulus that stimulates violence.

Even here, Shakespeare shows what we have just told. In one play after another, he dramatizes how it is possible to prevent potential or threatened violence, or to put an end to ongoing violence or at least limit it to nonphysical forms – as in *Measure for Measure*, *The Winter's Tale*,

---

[1] Freud (1961); Lorenz (1974).

The Tempest, and even *The Merchant of Venice*. As I (James Gilligan) found, it was possible to reduce lethal violence from war-zone levels to zero in the prisons of Massachusetts, lethal and nonlethal violence to zero in the jails of San Francisco, and rates of violent reoffending to zero or near-zero after release from incarceration in both institutional settings[2] – which it would not be possible to do any more than we could prevent the wish to eat, drink, and reproduce, if violence were truly instinctual. Shakespeare's dramatic portrayal of the ability of humane behavior to prevent violence is thus in line with current clinical/empirical evidence.

People who have had a relatively healthy, life-supporting upbringing will develop the capacity to experience and be sensitive to all of these feelings – shame and guilt as well as love. In fact, they are likely to reexperience these feelings each time they enter a new stage of development or maturation and face the challenges of that stage. When they solve the problems they confront, they demonstrate the emotional capacity that transcends both shame and guilt and removes the causes of both feelings and hence the causes of violence toward self and others: namely, the capacity to love both themselves and others (and to help others do the same). As we have mentioned, Shakespeare shows us this in Prospero in *The Tempest*, in Polixenes in *The Winter's Tale*, and in Duke Vincentio in *Measure for Measure*, among other plays.

Working in the prisons of Massachusetts made it possible to witness this sequence of emotional progression in the most violent of men. These were men who had committed extreme violence, up to and including multiple or serial murders, in response to feeling "disrespected" or "dissed" (shamed) by their victims or others (sometimes a lifetime of others, for whom their victims were merely the scapegoats). Their violence was a way of undoing their shame by transferring it from themselves to their victims, by showing that they were more powerful than their victims and could thus shame them instead. (The Latin roots of two of the words that refer to violence – assault and injury – both mean insult, among other meanings: so to assault or injure someone is to insult them – i.e., shame them. Thus one does not need to "add insult to injury": it is already right there, in the meaning of the word itself.)

After these incarcerated violent men were exposed, typically for the first time in their lives, to people who were interested enough in them to want to hear the story of their lives and would listen to those stories and attempt to understand them respectfully rather than judgmentally, the men became

---

[2] Gilligan and Lee (2004); Gilligan and Lee (2005); Lee and Gilligan (2005).

able to attain an understanding and a catharsis of the shame that had motivated their murderous behavior. By a combination of individual or group psychotherapy, and gaining access to nonviolent sources of pride and self-esteem, notably, education (up to and including college degrees), such men became able to develop a conscience and the capacity to feel guilty. In time, this enabled them to empathize with others enough to recognize how much suffering they had caused them. At that point, however, many would feel so guilty they would feel they deserved to die; some would even make suicide attempts, sometimes fatal, to punish themselves for their guilt. Thus our work with them would then have to focus on learning how to help them overcome their suicidality.

In the course of this work, it became clear that there was one thing and one thing only that enabled these men to outgrow their suicidal impulses and find their lives, even in prison, worth living. This happened when a man realized that he could be helpful and useful to other people – mostly, to a fellow prisoner or prisoners. One man taught the illiterate how to read and write; one helped others to write letters home; another helped others to navigate the prison's law library and write their legal briefs or petitions; one helped to improve the quality of the food service in the kitchen. That is how they became able to love both themselves and others.

One man who worked as a pimp in Boston's red-light district had killed several people in the community, so he was incarcerated in the Charles Street Jail in Boston to await his trial for murder. However, he killed another inmate in the jail, so he was transferred to the state's maximum security prison to await trial, even before being tried in court, since he was considered too dangerous to await trial in the jail. But he then killed yet another person in that prison, so he was transferred to the prison psychiatric hospital, whose purpose was treatment, not punishment. At first, he seemed untreatable: he was mute and so paranoid that we felt he would consider any attempt to approach him as violating the space he felt he needed from others. Our main goal was simply to keep everyone safe, by enabling him to feel safe. He could sleep in a bedroom behind a locked door, and during the day we kept everyone – staff and patients – from getting too close to him.

However, after a few months, during which his needs were treated with respect rather than condemnation or punishment, he took a young man with profound intellectual disabilities under his protection, accompanying him to and from the dining hall, so that this vulnerable youth would not be assaulted or harmed, physically or psychologically, by any of the other patients. Following this means of entering the human community (not reentering it, but joining it for the first time), he became ready to start talking about the events in his life, beginning with terrifying traumatic experiences throughout his childhood that had led him to where he was at this point. He then volunteered to do work in the hospital that benefited that whole community – so he not only became totally nonviolent himself (he has never even attempted to harm anyone again); he also succeeded in reducing the level of violence committed by others in the hospital.

Among people who are violent, the capacity to love others is a prerequisite for feeling guilty about the wish to harm them. That is, the capacity for ambivalence is a prerequisite for having guilt feelings, for one would not wish to hurt or destroy others unless one hated them, but would not feel guilty about having that wish unless one also loved them, as Shakespeare shows us in the story of Othello.

In sum, the feeling of shame (lack of self-love) is always accompanied by the feeling of innocence (the lack of self-hate). And the feeling of guilt (self-hate) is always accompanied by the feeling of pride (self-love). This is so because pride is caused by the feeling of being powerful, not weak, and guilt is caused by the fear that one is powerful enough to injure or kill others. Therefore, as we noted in the previous chapter, feelings of pride are a prerequisite for feelings of guilt, and the feeling of guilt is always accompanied by the feeling of pride. In the sin- and guilt-motivated moral value system of Christianity, pride is the deadliest of the Seven Deadly Sins, and the feeling of humility (self-humiliation) is considered the highest virtue.

Shame Ethics versus Guilt Ethics

Shame and guilt (and pride and innocence) are the moral emotions in that they are the *affective* components of what we can call, paraphrasing William James, "the varieties of moral experience." On the other hand, moral value systems – the value judgments, definitions, and preferences as to what constitutes good and evil, or justice and injustice, and the moral commandments as to what one should do or not do – are the *cognitive* content of moral experience. Just as shame and guilt are equal but opposite and antagonistic emotive and motive forces, they motivate two equal and opposite moral value systems, which we call shame ethics versus guilt ethics.

Shame ethics is a moral value system in which the worst evil is shame and humiliation, or disgrace and dishonor; and the highest good – the *summum bonum* – is the opposite, namely, pride and honor. Guilt ethics, by contrast, is a moral value system in which pride, far from being the highest good, is the worst evil: it is the deadliest of the Seven Deadly Sins, in the guilt ethic of Christianity. And humility, or self-humiliation, far from being the worst evil, is the highest good. In the guilt ethic of Christianity, as St. Augustine summarized it, "Humility is the foundation of all the other virtues; hence, in the soul in which this virtue does not exist there cannot be any other virtue." And "It was pride that changed angels into devils; it is humility that makes men as angels."[3] Seen in this light, these two ethical value systems are the same, except that what is given a positive value in the one is given a negative value in the other.

This distinction and the claim that there are two moral value systems have been anticipated by many observers of moral psychology. St. Augustine, for example, contrasted the ethos of the Roman Empire with that of Christianity: "The glory with the desire of which the Romans burned is the judgment of men thinking well of men. [But] virtue is better, which is content with no human judgment save that of one's own conscience. Whence the apostle says, 'For this is our glory, the testimony of our conscience.'"[4]

Milton contrasted the ethic of God with that of Lucifer (the latter of which he summarizes as "Evil, be thou my good"). Nietzsche contrasted what he called "master morality" (the ethic of the *Iliad*, the Roman empire, feudal Japan, slave-owners, and of himself, whom he identifies as the Anti-Christ) with "slave morality" (the ethic of Jesus, who said we should be servants to each other, resist not evil, etc.).

Thorstein Veblen contrasted the ethics of capitalism (what we are calling shame ethics) with those of Christianity (guilt ethics.)[5] In *The Moral Judgment of the Child*, Piaget's study of the evolution from one morality to another during the course of child development, he called them heteronomous-gerontocratic morality (early childhood, where moral values and commandments are seen to emanate from other people who have more power, including the power to punish, i.e., the parents, so that "might" is what is "right") and autonomous-democratic morality (from middle childhood on, in which morality increasingly emanates from one's conscience or from the social contract of the group, in this case, agreement among children as to the rules of the game, how they are made, and how they can be changed – a democratic rather than authoritarian

---

[3] *Humilitas homines sanctis angelis similes facit, et superbia ex angelis demones facit.* As quoted in *Manipulus Florum* (c. 1306), ed. Thomas Hibernicus, *Superbia i cum uariis.* See the Electronic Manipulus florum: www.manipulusflorum.com.

[4] St. Augustine, *The City of God*, Book V, Chapter 12.

[5] Veblen (1910), p. 185: "there is . . . much that makes for an effectual discrepancy between the two."

system).[6] Adorno et al. and subsequent psychologists and psychoanalysts have contrasted authoritarian ("potentially fascist") with egalitarian (social-democratic) beliefs and behaviors, noting that authoritarian personalities are hypersensitive to shame and hyposensitive to guilt, whereas the opposite is true of those who are egalitarian and democratic.[7] The psychoanalyst Heinz Hartmann contrasted narcissistic (shame-driven) with compulsive-imperativistic (guilt-sensitive) ethics.[8] And the psychologist Sylvan Tomkins found right-wing (hierarchical) political ideologies and value systems to be motivated by the wish to undo or avoid feelings of shame, whereas left-wing (egalitarian) political values and ideologies focused more on the wish to avoid the guilt of subjecting others to a level of social status, economic affluence, and political power that was inferior to what they themselves enjoyed. Thus left-wing politics appeared to be motivated more by placing the highest value on humility, equality, and democracy, rather than on superiority and hierarchy, such as patriarchy (male supremacy) or racial prejudice (white supremacy).[9]

Yet among those who have noticed or made this distinction between two contrasting forms of morality, law and politics, we prioritize Shakespeare, because he alone brought these value distinctions to life with great specificity and detail and in an immense variety of different contexts and circumstances, in the words and actions of the characters he depicted in his plays. For example, for Hamlet, "Thou shalt not kill," as Judeo-Christian guilt ethics commands, vies with "Thou shalt kill" as the shame ethic that the ghost, his father, invoked, and commanded Hamlet to obey. As a result, Hamlet is paralyzed. He is caught between two diametrically opposite moral value systems, one of which commands the avoidance of guilt and sin, which it identifies with killing, and the other of which commands murder, as the only means by which to restore the father's honor and undo his shame. Both value systems had coexisted for centuries as central components of the moral traditions of the culture in which Hamlet lived (and as he repeatedly expressed, he was profoundly sensitive to both emotions, shame and guilt). Hence, he was paralyzed.

To put it simply, what we call immoral are whatever behaviors or motivations we feel are shameful or guilt-inducing. And as Shakespeare dramatizes, there are two moral value systems: one caused by the emotions

---

[6] Piaget (1965).

[7] Adorno et al. (1950); Altemeyer (1981); Altemeyer (1996). In fact, the highest scorers in Adorno et al.'s scale for measuring the degree of potential fascism, or right-wing extremism, were violent criminals in San Quentin Prison.

[8] Hartmann (1960).   [9] Tomkins (1995).

of shame versus pride and honor, the other by its opposite, the feelings of guilt versus innocence (self-righteousness).

It was among incarcerated men that these dynamics became not only observable but surprising. And because these dynamics are relevant to our discussion of Shakespeare, we will take a moment to follow the path that led us to these insights. When I (James Gilligan) first began working as a psychiatrist with violent prisoners, I assumed the validity of what I had been taught up to that point, and what many people believe: namely, that people who commit the kinds of actions that cause them to land in prison are simply "amoral." That is, that they had never developed a moral value system, which is why they committed their heinous crimes. To my astonishment, the opposite turned out to be true. I had never encountered a group of people who were more dedicated to morality: more than I or any of my friends or colleagues were. They were willing to go to their deaths – and often did – in order to stand up for their moral principles. They were obsessed with issues of fairness and unfairness, justice and injustice, meaning how they had been treated unfairly and unjustly since childhood by parents and then by others in the community, by prison guards or their fellow prison inmates, or by members of other racial, religious, or ethnic groups.

These experiences led me to the conclusion that perceiving oneself as a victim of injustice causes feelings of shame (and therefore also innocence), which motivates violence against others; whereas perceiving oneself as a perpetrator of injustice (the opposite of how almost all violent prisoners judged themselves) causes feelings of guilt (of which an inextricable component is the feeling of pride), which motivates a need for self-punishment, or violence against the self. To carry the point further, the men who committed violent crimes were in fact disproportionately the victims of what a guilt ethic would call injustice; that is, the most violent among them were often the victims of life-threatening violence or even attempted murder by one or both parents, or were the survivors of a parent or sibling or other close relative who had been murdered, often in front of their eyes. Or they were the victims of other forms of child abuse: sexual abuse, psychological/emotional abuse, or the deadliest of all: neglect and abandonment. And they were also disproportionately the victims of another form of what a guilt ethic would call injustice, such as racial prejudice and discrimination; poverty; unequal access to education, employment, health care, and political power; invidious treatment by the law enforcement and criminal justice system; and so on. Their adherence to a shame ethic was the inevitable and in its own way "rational" and "defensible" response to being treated in a way that could not without hypocrisy be defended by those who claimed to believe in a guilt ethic – although their behavior led to suffering and often death, for their victims and for themselves as well.

Among the most radically illuminating dramatizations in Shakespeare's plays, and perhaps the most frequently overlooked, is that morality does not prevent violence. What Shakespeare shows us and what we are setting out to tell in this book is quite the contrary: morality stimulates violence. And by doing so, it causes deaths. The paradox here is that what we call morality (as defined by moral value systems, value judgments, and commandments) has been handed down to us a means of preventing violence; whereas in fact morality stimulates violence – toward others as shame ethics does, or toward oneself, as guilt ethics commands.

What, then, can actually prevent violence? Again, Shakespeare shows us the answer: love. Love toward self and others. For where love exists, morality, meaning moral value judgments and commandments, becomes irrelevant, redundant, and unnecessary. As Aristotle put it, "if men are friends [*philon*] there is no need for justice [*dikaiosunes*] between them; whereas merely to be just is not enough" (*Nicomachean Ethics*, VIII.i.4). Jesus said much the same when he said, "When you have done everything that was *commanded* you [by the moral law], you ought to say 'We are useless slaves, we have done [only] what we were *obliged* to do'" (Luke 17:10). To paraphrase, love is much more generous than morality and hence love transcends morality, making it not only unnecessary but stingy, leading Hume to speak of justice as the "cautious, jealous virtue."[10]

Kant also saw how love makes moral value judgments and commandments unnecessary and redundant: as he put it, if "we are conscious of liking to do" what the moral law commands us to do, "a command would be quite needless."[11] And as he also saw, "Affection towards men is possible no doubt, but cannot be commanded, for it is not in the power of any man to love anyone at command." And while "Duty and obligation are the only names that we must give to our relation to the moral law," it is also true that "all duty is necessitation or constraint. But what is done from constraint is not done from love." He adds, "It is a very beautiful thing to do good to men from love to them and from sympathetic good will . . .; but this is not . . . the true moral maxim of our conduct." In short, we need morality because, and only because, being humans and not angels or

---

[10] Hume (1951), III.ii.2, p. 495; Hume (1975), III.i.145, p. 184.
[11] Kant (1952), Part I, Book I, Chapter III, p. 326.

saints, our capacity for love is limited and we often wish to do things that would be expressions of either hate or indifference rather than of love – toward others, or toward ourselves.

There are two problems with morality, however. The first is that morality, which came into existence to compensate for the limitation of our capacity for love, actually inhibits that capacity. This insight, though not insisted on and not apparently even consciously recognized, is nevertheless ineluctably implied by several of the classical commentators on the relationship between love and morality (and specifically, moral worth or desert). For example, Kant notes in his discussion of Christ's commandment to love that "we must make the sad remark that our species, alas! is not such as to be found particularly *worthy* of love when we know it more closely."[12] Freud, likewise, objected to Christ's commandment "for a universal love of mankind" on two moral grounds: first, "a love that does not discriminate ... [does] an *injustice* to its object; and secondly, not all men are *worthy* of love."[13] But it was perhaps Shakespeare who summed up the antagonism between moral value judgments and love (both of neighbor and of self) most powerfully when he had Hamlet exclaim: "Use all men after their *deserts* and who would 'scape *whipping?*"[14] Here he is saying in effect that moral value judgments (having to do with what one deserves, according to moral criteria) lead to the withdrawal of love and the infliction of violent punishment (whipping). So moral value systems, which we humans rely on to compensate for the limitations in our capacity to love, actually inhibit that capacity.

In short, the stricter the moral standards by which people judge themselves and others, the more strongly they will be inhibited from loving those same people. Specifically, shame ethics inhibits the capacity for love of others (altruism) in order to reserve love for the self; but the higher the standards and level of aspiration for achievement and power which a given person has incorporated into their shame ethic, the more impossible it will be for the person to satisfy those standards and feel self-love (pride). Correspondingly, the stricter a person's guilt ethic is, the more strongly it will prohibit what it calls "selfishness" and inhibit the capacity for self-love (pride). But by the same token, as Kant, Freud, and Shakespeare revealed in the remarks just quoted, other people will also fail to live up to standards high enough to make them morally "worthy" of love either.

---

[12] Ibid., p. 370 (emphasis added). [13] Freud (1961), p. 102 (emphasis added).
[14] Emphasis added.

The second problem with morality is that while it ostensibly serves the purpose of promoting beneficent behavior and thus protecting and enhancing people's lives, welfare, and happiness, it actually motivates the destruction of people's lives, welfare, and happiness. Shame ethics motivates the destruction of other people (and often, as noted above, of oneself as well); and guilt ethics motivates the destruction of one's own life (and sometimes, as noted above, of others' as well). Or, to be more exact, the ultimate goal and deepest wish that guilt motivates is not the welfare of others but the elimination of the feeling of guilt; and that is achieved most directly by self-punishment and self-sacrifice, which may indirectly but ineluctably entail harm to others as well – especially, for example, those who are dependent on oneself, and who can therefore only be harmed by the self-sacrifice of the person on whom they are dependent.

Shame and Guilt Cultures

The anthropological concept of shame cultures and guilt cultures and the contrast between them dates back at least to Ruth Benedict's 1946 classic: *The Chrysanthemum and the Sword: Patterns of Culture.* As Benedict observes:

> A society that inculcates absolute standards of morality and relies on men's developing a conscience is a guilt culture by definition, but a man in such a society may, as in the United States, suffer in addition from shame when he accuses himself of gaucheries which are in no way sins. He may be exceedingly chagrined about not dressing appropriately for the occasion or about a slip of the tongue.…
>
> True shame cultures rely on external sanctions for good behavior, not, as true guilt cultures do, on an internalized conviction of sin. Shame is a reaction to other people's criticism. A man is shamed either by being openly ridiculed and rejected or by fantasying to himself that he has been ridiculous. In either case it is a potent sanction. But it requires an audience or at least a man's fantasy of an audience. Guilt does not.[15]

Benedict had earlier developed an anthropological theory of shame cultures in her summary and paraphrase of observations that her mentor Franz Boas had made during his fieldwork with the Kwakiutl, an Amerindian people on Vancouver Island. The Kwakiutl competed for pride and prestige by means of what they called a "potlatch," which corresponded closely to what Thorstein Veblen described in an

---

[15] Benedict (1946), pp. 222–3.

American context as the conspicuous consumption and conspicuous waste by which the "robber barons" of the late nineteenth century competed for status and prestige (like the robber barons of today).[16] In a manner roughly reminiscent of what Shakespeare dramatizes in *Timon of Athens*, the Kwakiutl used competitive conspicuous displays of wealth and power to demonstrate and validate their own superiority over their less affluent competitors.

The anthropologist Michelle Rosaldo developed the theory of shame cultures further through her study of New Guinea tribes, in which she argued that "of all themes in the literature on culture and personality, the opposition between guilt and shame has probably proven most resilient."[17] With respect to violence, pure and extreme shame cultures place a positive value on aggressiveness toward others (war, murder, torture, theft, enslavement, and social and economic inequalities) and do not inculcate or even recognize either the feeling or the concept of guilt. The Kwakiutl, for example, as Boas[18] and Benedict[19] described, engaged in headhunting, cannibalism, burning slaves alive, and undiscriminating, merciless war and murder against even totally innocent, unsuspecting, hospitable, sleeping friends, neighbors, relatives, or hosts – adults and children. Furthermore, it seems clear that the motive for this aggression was the desire to minimize or wipe out feelings of shame, humiliation, and "loss of face," and to maximize feelings of pride and the attainment of social prestige. Aggressive behavior was a recognized and honored way of doing this. As Ruth Benedict writes,[20] "all accidents were occasions upon which one was shamed ... Death was the paramount affront they recognized.... They took recognized means ... to wipe out the shame" – such as killing a neighboring chief in order to wipe out the shame of having suffered a death in one's own family. While this illustrates the principle that it is less painful to feel angry than it is to feel shamed, it also shows that it is less painful to feel angry than to feel sad.

An approach to quantifying the concept and description of shame cultures has been made by Slater and Slater (1965), who surveyed the cross-cultural literature as summarized in the Human Relations Area Files,[21] and extracted five characteristics of "narcissism" (a synonym for shame) in cultures, and a summation of the five, which they called a "composite narcissism index." They found that cultures that had characteristics definitive of shame cultures also exhibited extremes of both

[16] Veblen (1953).   [17] Rosaldo (1983), p. 135.   [18] Boas (1966).   [19] Benedict (1958).
[20] Ibid.   [21] Textor (1972).

violence and social inequality with a frequency that was highly statistically significant (i.e., would occur by chance less than once in a hundred times). The shame-related categories included "Extreme sensitivity to insult," "Boastfulness," "Invidious display of wealth," and a "Composite narcissism index." In every culture ranked high in these characteristics, "warfare is prevalent." And all of them also ranked high in other varieties of violent behavior, such as "killing, torturing or mutilation of the enemy," "extreme bellicosity (high incidence of wars, raids, homicidal vendettas, violent aggression toward surrounding tribes, and other evidence of belligerence and warlikeness)," "strong or moderate emphasis on military glory," "incidence of personal [violent] crime," "alcoholic aggression," and early socialization practices that permitted, disinhibited, or actively encouraged aggressive behavior.

Shame cultures, as defined by the criteria noted above, also have hierarchical, authoritarian, ethnocentric social structures and values that divide people into superior versus inferior grades of socioeconomic status, with wide variations of social class and caste, prestige, wealth, and power. These distinctions separate the population into aristocrats, commoners, and slaves. The hierarchies in terms of which shame cultures divide their populations into superior and inferior in modern societies include those of socioeconomic class, caste, ethnicity, religion, gender, and age. In the age of feudalism, which was just ending during Shakespeare's lifetime, serfs were the equivalent of slaves; and two and a half centuries after Shakespeare's time, chattel slaves were replaced by what Marx called "wage slaves."

To the extent that any given society is a shame culture, its political psychology requires hierarchy and a lowest class, what has been called a *lumpenproletariat* or "underclass," and relies on what I (David Richards), have called "moral slavery," a structural stigmatizing that rationalizes shaming and scapegoating of those assigned to the inferior status. Shame cultures are found in the cross-cultural surveys just cited to be significantly more likely to stratify their population into upper versus lower socioeconomic classes and castes, masters versus slaves, aristocrats versus commoners, invidious displays of wealth, and the possession and inheritance of private property. Patriarchy, because it is founded on a gender binary and gender hierarchy, similarly bears the markings of a shame culture. Thus, the perceived shaming of manhood (the casting of any doubt on a man's masculinity, his sexual adequacy as a man, even in areas of behavior that are not literally "sexual") does not merely permit or justify his resorting to violence, it requires it – as the only means, ultimately, for him to prove that he is a man, and a sexually adequate one at that.

Extreme guilt cultures[22] are classless, democratic, and communistic, with an equal sharing of prestige, power, and wealth. Competition, such as it is, is more likely to be for the highest degree of humility than for prestige and honor. As for violence, one such culture, the Hutterites, an Anabaptist sect that practices a way of life modeled on strict adherence to the New Testament, experienced not a single homicide, assault, or rape during their first seventy-five years of existence in the United States (from the late nineteenth to the mid-twentieth centuries), nor did they have any need for a police force; and many Hutterites spent time in federal prisons (some were even tortured and murdered there by the US federal government, during World War I), because, as strict pacifists, they refused to kill people for the US military.[23] Their only lethal violence during that entire period of more than eight decades was against themselves: two or possibly three suicides. Extreme guilt cultures, such as this one, institutionalize confession of sins as a means of relieving guilt (and, of course, that increases shame – which is one of the reasons that it decreases guilt), whereas in shame cultures, exposure of transgressions of social mores is avoided and concealment of them is sought. Hence the prevalence of lying, deception, and fraud as means of avoiding shame, in people and cultures that are especially sensitive to feelings of shame.

In sum, shame and guilt ethics are the ethos, the moral value system, of shame and guilt cultures, respectively.

The stunning relevance of Shakespeare to our analysis of shame and guilt follows from the observation that tragedy is the literary form in which guilt cultures and guilt ethics critique the shame cultures and guilt ethics that preceded them. Not only that, they do so by showing the enormity of the violence, death, destruction, and suffering that shame cultures cause, both to individuals and to societies. Seen in this light, the invention of tragedy is a sign or signal of the transition from a shame to a guilt culture. This occurred first in fifth-century Athens with the great Greek tragedies and then again in Elizabethan England, with the reinvention of tragedy as a literary form. As Zevedei Barbu[24] put it, "Cannot the rise of tragedy itself, with its centred motive of guilt and expiation, be taken as symptomatic ...? One wonders indeed whether

---

[22] An example would be the Hutterites, a strictly pacifistic Anabaptist community in the northern United States and southern Canada which models its way of life on that of the earliest Christian communities, including the communal sharing of wealth, or "primitive Christian communism," as described in *The Acts of the Apostles.* See Eaton and Weil (1955); Kaplan and Plaut (1956); Hostetler and Huntington (1967).

[23] Hostetler and Huntington (1967).   [24] Barbu (1960), p. 106.

the birth of tragedy in any civilization is not a symptom of guilt-culture, or of the beginning of guilt-culture."

Shame and Guilt in History

In *The Greeks and the Irrational*, the classics scholar Eric Dodds, drawing on Ruth Benedict's definitions, documented the transition in Greek history from an earlier shame culture (the society depicted in *The Iliad*) to a later guilt culture (classical Athens at the time of the tragedians and the philosophers).[25] Speaking of "the uninhibited boasting in which Homeric man indulges," Dodds says that

> Homeric man's highest good is not the enjoyment of a quiet conscience, but the enjoyment of *time*, public esteem [honor].... And the strongest moral force which Homeric man knows is not the fear of god, but respect for public opinion, *aidos* [shame or sense of shame and honor, meaning sensitivity to shame and dishonor]. In such a society, anything which exposes a man to the contempt or ridicule of his fellows, which causes him to "lose face," is felt as unbearable.

By the time the Greeks became a guilt culture, however, they worried not about experiencing too little pride and prestige, but too much – overweening pride or arrogance, up to and including violence – for which they used the term *hubris*. Far from being the highest good, pride by this time was called the "prime evil" (*proton kakon*), as Theognis called it; the *hamartia*, or tragic flaw, for which, in Aristotle's analysis, Sophocles' Oedipus punished himself. It is significant that in the earlier shame culture's version of the Oedipus myth, as alluded to in the *Iliad*, Oedipus, far from feeling guilty and self-punitive, continued to reign in Thebes and was eventually buried with royal honors.[26]

Probably the individual who symbolized this transition to a guilt culture most vividly was Socrates, who declared that it was better to be a victim of injustice than a perpetrator of it, and who finally committed suicide,

---

[25] Dodds (1959), pp. 17–18.

[26] Dodds (1951), pp. 36, 55. "We get a further measure of the gap [between the shame-centered values of the Homeric shame culture and the later guilt culture of classical Athens] if we compare Homer's version of the Oedipus saga with that familiar to us from Sophocles [which was of course the version on which Freud built his explanation of the source of guilt feelings]. In the latter, Oedipus becomes a polluted outcast, crushed under the burden of a guilt 'which neither the earth nor the holy rain nor the sunlight can accept.' But in the story Homer knew he continues to reign in Thebes after his guilt is discovered, and is eventually killed in battle and buried with royal honors" (p. 36).

choosing to be a victim of the injustice of the Athenians, even when he could easily have escaped from it.

For the most extreme development of guilt in the ethos of a culture, however, we must turn to Judeo-Christian culture. Many scholars have made this observation. Freud, for example, commented that "the people of Israel ... out of their sense of guilt ... created the over-strict commandments of their priestly religion."[27] And Nietzsche saw that "the arrival of the Christian God ... has brought with it the phenomenon of the uttermost sense of guilt."[28] And we have already noticed that the earliest extant description of the difference between a shame and a guilt culture was written by one of the early Christian thinkers, St. Augustine. The greater intensity of guilt in Christian as compared with Greek culture is indicated by the growth in guilt-affective tone of the word *hamartia*, from "tragic flaw" (the usual translation of Aristotle's meaning) to "sin," the New Testament meaning of the word. And of course St. Augustine's doctrine of original sin (which Hamlet paraphrased in saying, "use every man after his deserts and who would 'scape whipping?") made it clear that you could not be a Christian without accepting that we are all guilty, or sinful. Or as Jesus put it, no man is good, only God is good (Matt. 10:17).

Like Socrates, Christ became a personal symbol for the values of a guilt culture, becoming a victim rather than a perpetrator of violence (and severely chastising his followers when they were ready to defend him). This does not necessarily indicate any great difference between early Christianity and the religious and moral values of major portions of the Jewish community at that same time, for Jesus was, after all, a rabbi, and most verses of the "Sermon on the Mount" have rabbinical precedent.[29] In other words, Christianity began as a subculture within the larger religious culture of the Judaism of his time.

It is worth noting, however, that the Judeo-Christian tradition, like the Greek one, began as a shame culture and only later developed into an extreme guilt culture. The earliest moral emotion mentioned in the Bible, for example, immediately after Adam and Eve have eaten the fruit of the tree of the knowledge of good and evil, is the "shame" they felt over being naked. Their children then demonstrate how shame stimulates violence: Cain kills his brother Abel because God "had respect unto Abel and his offering, but unto Cain and his offering God had not respect." In other words, Cain kills Abel because he felt disrespected, or "dissed" – exactly the reason contemporary murderers give as to why they had to kill someone.

[27] Freud (1961), p. 127.   [28] Nietzsche (2004), p. 66.   [29] Buttrick (2002).

What is unique about Judaism, however, is how early and strongly the theme of guilt (called sin) emerged. Although in the earlier books of the Hebrew Bible, God commands the Jewish people to commit genocide against their enemies, stone to death adulterous women, and so on, and the Jewish leaders pray to God to help them succeed in putting their enemies to shame, by the time of the later books the moral exhortations of the Prophets warn against the sinfulness of pride, violence, injustice, and neglect of the poor, until the latter theme finally drowns out the former. The parallelism between Greek and Jewish culture – first a shame culture, then a guilt culture – together with the apparently much wider distribution of shame than of guilt cultures throughout the world, suggests the possibility that there is a general trend for cultures, like individuals, to be sensitive to shame before they are to guilt, but also that cultures can progress from being shame-dominated to being guilt-sensitive.

However, the history of Christianity also illustrates another possibility – the regression of a culture from a guilt into a shame culture. During its first three centuries of existence, Christianity existed under conditions that would appeal to guilt-ridden people – namely, persecution and martyrdom. Early Christianity fit Nietzsche's description of slave morality, since it identified with slaves and the qualities necessary to be slaves, such as meekness, passivity, and submissiveness in the face of domination and exploitation (advice it gave to those who literally were slaves, as well as to the free). But it also did the opposite: that is, far from enslaving anyone themselves, the early Christians were remarkably egalitarian, sharing their wealth equally among the whole community, in what has been called "primitive Christian communism": that is, from each according to their ability, to each according to their need (Acts 2:44–5).

However, with the conversion of the Emperor Constantine early in the fourth century, Christianity became the religion of the masters, not the slaves or the poor; and the motives for becoming a Christian reversed accordingly. Thus Christianity changed from being a relatively pure and extreme guilt culture to a mixed, but primarily shame-dominated culture, capable of inspiring extremes not only of masochism, as formerly, but also of sadism; of martyrdom and murder, saintliness and savagery, piety and power, and pacifism and genocide – Francis of Assisi and Torquemada. The Crusades in which people who called themselves Christians slaughtered Muslims and others were only among the most extreme of the atrocities committed in the name of the Prince of Peace. The earlier self-sacrificing guilt culture of Christianity survived, or was revived, in only a few atypical pockets of extreme religious fervor, such as some monastic communities and, after the Reformation, in some Anabaptist religious guilt cultures such as the strictly pacifist Hutterites, Mennonites, and Amish, or in firmly pacifist denominations such as the Quakers.

What this illustrates, however, is that people who are experiencing guilt (a precondition for which is that they have already attained feelings of pride) are motivated to identify with the underdogs, such as the slaves, in order to reduce their pride and hence their guilt. However, those who have not yet overcome their feelings of shame (i.e., they still feel weak and inferior) are motivated to identify with the "overdog" – or as Nietzsche put it, the "overman" or "superman," the *Ubermensch*, the slave-owners or slave-masters, or as the Nazis put it, the "master race" – in order to increase their feelings of pride, power, and superiority.

The relevance of all this to Shakespeare is this: given that tragedy, historically, has been the literary form in which guilt cultures criticize shame cultures (just as epic poetry – the Homeric poems, the Aeneid, the Icelandic sagas, etc. – are the form in which shame cultures celebrate themselves), Shakespeare shows us why the guilt culture that was just coming into being during his lifetime became motivated to repudiate the shame culture that preceded it. He dramatizes the costs of shame ethics not only in his tragedies but also in his history plays. For example, in *1 Henry IV*, with the character of Falstaff, Shakespeare deconstructs the concept of "honor" in a hilarious comic monologue. Thus he turns the most powerful weapon in the arsenal of shame cultures, namely, ridicule, against a central concept in shame cultures' own ethos:

> honour pricks on. Yes, but how if honour prick me off when I come on? Can honour set to a let? No. Or an arm? No. Or take away the grief of a wound? No. Honour hath no skill in surgery, then? No. What is honour? A word. What is in that word "honour"? What is that "honour"? Air. A trim reckoning. Who hath it? He that died o'Wednesday. Doth he feel it? No. Doth he hear it? No. 'Tis insensible than? Yea, to the dead. But will it not live with the living? No. Why? Detraction will not suffer it. There I'll none of it. Honour is a mere scutcheon. And so ends my catechism. (*1 Henry IV*, V.i.126–40)

And in *Hamlet*, Shakespeare again points out how absurd it is to go to war for the sake of honor, in which whole armies "go to gain a little patch of ground / That hath in it no profit but the name," and risking the lives of thousands of soldiers "Even for an egg-shell," and "to find quarrel in a straw when honor's at the stake." Honor thus leads "twenty thousand men ... for a fantasy and a trick of fame" to "Go to their graves like beds," and to "fight for a plot" of land "Which is not tomb enough and continent / To hide the slain," that is, not large enough to bury the quantity of men who will be killed (V.iv.18–65).

Hamlet's tragedy, however, is that while he cannot rationally defend that ethic, he is also unable to escape it: he has one leg in the shame ethic of his father's and Fortinbras' shame culture, which commands both individual and mass murder for the sake of honor, and another in the not yet completely dead nor yet fully resurrected guilt culture with which to replace the shame culture and its ethos of "honor through violence." Thus he was left with no credible moral value system with which to guide his behavior. As he puts it, "the time is out of joint: / O cursed spite, that I was born to set it right."

Shame-Dominated versus Guilt-Sensitive Legal and Political Systems

In his plays, Shakespeare shows us the enormous violence, death, and destruction that was caused by the hierarchical political system of his day – monarchy – and the shame culture that engendered and validated that system. And while it is true that he at no point evoked the kind of political system called democracy – it was not even one of the political possibilities during his lifetime – it does seem to us that the power of his critique of monarchy could hardly have left his audience without the incentive to try to imagine a less shame-provoking and violent political system, in which political power and regime change would be decided not by violence but by nonviolent means, such as persuasion, argument, reason, evidence, and noncoerced choice – in other words, democracy. And indeed, in the first generation after Shakespeare, Great Britain began an evolution, which is still going on throughout many nations (though not without constant conflict and many defeats and regressions) toward a more and more democratic system. With the growth of a more secular, skeptical, scientific mentality beginning in the seventeenth century, the traditional source of legitimacy of the system of monarchy, namely, the "divine right of kings," began to lose its credibility – for without a divinity, how can there be a "divine right"? This trend began with the populist, quasi-democratic, and still religiously rationalized revolution that resulted in the beheading of Charles I in 1649, and then by the eventual transformation of the British monarchy from an autocracy into the constitutional monarchy it is today in an otherwise democratic and secular political system. In France, the United States, and many other Western nations (and, more recently, some

Asian ones as well, such as Japan and South Korea), monarchy has been replaced by more or less democratic, egalitarian, and secular political and economic systems.

With the end of feudalism, the middle ages, hierarchical (post-Constantinian) Christendom, and "the age of faith," the legal system similarly became less and less moralistic, punitive, and violent. This is illustrated by the trend in all modern democracies (with the sole exception of the United States) toward the partial or complete abolition of so-called retributive justice: inhumane conditions of confinement, from life-threatening extremes of temperature (physical torture) to years or even decades of uninterrupted solitary confinement (psychological torture), life sentences, and capital punishment, among many other means of inflicting pain or death. Shakespeare, however, did envision and dramatize what a government could look like when its criminal justice system was no longer bloodthirsty and sadistic. In several plays, he shows us rulers who replace "retributive justice" (the euphemism for punishment, revenge, and violence) with what today is called "restorative justice" – namely, the rehabilitation, education, and therapy of violent or potentially violent offenders; their reconciliation with those they had offended against; and the acceptance of their return to the communities they had injured. Examples are *Measure for Measure*, *The Tempest*, and *The Winter's Tale*.

In a highly successful violence-prevention experiment in the jails of San Francisco, a central component was the replacement of the traditional model of retributive justice with restorative justice. In this "Resolve to Stop the Violence Project" (RSVP), violent offenders not only learned why they had been engaging in the violence that had, as they themselves came to see, ruined their lives as well as ruining or ending the lives of their victims; they spontaneously began doing what they could to restore to the community what they had taken from it, namely, a sense of safety, security, and trust. They became advocates, even therapists, themselves, devoted to helping new admissions to the jail make the same progress that they had made toward lives devoted to nonviolence and to healing; and then expanded that mission to similar work with actual or potential violent offenders in the community, after they were released from the jail. This experiment in violence prevention found that even as little as four months in the program reduced violent reoffending following release from the jails by more than 80 percent, and that in addition to making the community safer (the most important point), it also saved taxpayers $4 for every $1 spent on the program (given how much violent crime costs the whole community in purely financial terms).[30] Thus we might conclude, to say the least, that in dramatizing the need for replacing retributive with restorative justice, through such characters as the Duke in *Measure for Measure*, Shakespeare was on to something that it would be very valuable for us to learn and apply universally today.

[30] Gilligan and Lee (2005); Lee and Gilligan (2005); Schwartz (2009).

CHAPTER 2

The Cycle of Violence in the History Plays

Although often seen as paeans to honor and as celebrating the glories of military and political power, Shakespeare's history plays are in fact unsparing depictions of an endless cycle of violence. He shows us that when people pursue political power by means of violence (which today is called dictatorship) or seek justice by means of revenge (which today is called retributive justice), the result is more violence. In essence, the history plays offer a documentation of how violence simply engenders more violence. Starting with the deposing and murder of Richard II by Bolingbroke in *Richard II*, the plays trace a sequence of unending civil wars, in which violence is both an effect of previous violence and a cause of subsequent violence. Shakespeare dramatizes this throughout the plays *Richard II*, *Henry IV* (parts 1 and 2), *Henry V*, and *Henry VI* (parts 1–3), culminating in the murder, mayhem, and civil wars of *Richard III* that lead to his death, which is followed by Tudor absolutism, itself marked by an endless series of executions of political rivals.

Unlike the first tragedian, Aeschylus, who, in the *Oresteia*, depicts the replacement of a cycle of violence (family feuds and endless revenge and counter-revenge) by democracy and the rule of law, Shakespeare wrote at a time when democracy was not even among the range of political possibilities. Indeed, even the plays that deal with the quasi-democratic Roman Republic (*Julius Caesar* and *Coriolanus*) display mob violence, anarchy, and the destruction of democracy, rather than anything that could be called the rule of law. But monarchy (and aristocracy, with which it was intertwined) constituted the only possible political structure in Shakespeare's world, given who had power.

Nevertheless, his history plays show the problems created by hereditary monarchy and aristocracy as a political system. This includes the fact that political power and regime change, when contested, can be attained in those political structures only by means of constantly repeated cycles of violence, which are themselves often simply enlarged forms of family violence (since titles were normally accorded through familial inheritance, not individual achievement). Even though Shakespeare never says this explicitly (nor could he, given that criticism of the monarchy would have been a capital offense), it seems implicit in these plays that the only solution to the problems created by autocracy and aristocracy is democracy – since he also makes it clear that anarchy and mob violence are no solution. Indeed, that was exactly the conclusion the British people reached, not long after Shakespeare's death – that there were no feasible or viable alternatives to democracy – as they began the long, halting, sometimes reversed, and still-evolving journey toward a more and more democratic political system.

To say this is not to say that Shakespeare's plays are the reason the British people did this, but rather that Shakespeare, like poets everywhere, was a kind of super-sensitive "early warning system" capable of sensing the earliest stirrings in the *Zeitgeist*, the spirit of the times, in which he lived. Correspondingly, in addition to showing the almost limitless violence created by the system of hereditary monarchies, he did create a model of a kind of nonviolent rustic democracy – an equal sharing of power and wealth – in some of his comedies, romances, and "problem plays;" and he also anticipated and dramatized the replacement of retributive justice, or violent revenge, in both the political and the criminal justice realms, with what today is called restorative justice, as we will describe in Chapter 8.

So let us begin with Richard II. In response to being insulted by Bolingbroke, who has accused him of treason, Mowbray, the Duke of Norfolk, makes it clear that his honor, that is, his reputation, is more important to him than his life. When King Richard attempts to calm him, proclaiming that "Rage must be withstood," Mowbray responds:

> My life thou shalt command, but not my shame:
> The one my duty owes, but my fair name,
> Despite of death that lives upon my grave,
> To dark dishonor's use thou shalt not have.
> I am disgrac'd, impeached and baffled [accused and dishonored] here,
> Pierc'd to the soul with slander's venom'd spear,
> The which no balm can cure but his heart-blood
> Which breath'd this poison.

Mowbray here is making a distinction between his soul and his body; for, as he says, dishonor pierces the soul with venom and poison, from which the soul can survive only by means of one balm –the "heart-blood" of the person who dishonored him – even if that causes the death of his own bodily life.

He makes it clear that "honor" is synonymous with a spotless "reputation" – that is, what men think of other men – without which, even if his body survives, that is all that survives. His soul, his survival as a human being (a soul, a self, a person), rather than just a physical object, dies:

> The purest treasure mortal times afford
> Is spotless reputation; that away,
> Men are but gilded loam or painted clay.
> (I.i.177–8)

And he makes it clear that his honor, meaning the survival of his soul (his self), that is, his life *as a person, a human being*, is more important to him than mere *physical* survival:

> Mine honor is my life, both grow in one,
> Take honor from me, and my life is done.
> Then, dear my liege, mine honor let me try,
> In that I live, and for that I will die.
> (I.i.182–5)

In short, Mowbray would sacrifice his body in order to save his soul.

The Greek word for "soul," *psyche*, also means "life." So one is alive as a human being, meaning the possessor of a soul, only if one's soul is still alive. To lose one's soul is to suffer the death of one's self, one's uniquely human essence, which is dissociated here from the death of the *soma*, the body.

Mowbray is not speaking here figuratively. He is describing something that is literally true. This is not just exaggerated rhetoric or metaphor. The most violent men our society produces, the violent criminals in our prisons, tell us that they themselves had died, even before they started killing other people. What they mean by that is that they feel their personality has died, they feel dead and empty inside, they have lost the capacity for feelings, either emotional or physical, so that they feel numb and lifeless. This has led to concepts such as "death of the self"[1] and "soul murder,"[2] as opposed to death of the body. And these men could often specify the events or circumstances that had caused the death of their self: uniformly, it was an experience of feeling shamed, humiliated, rejected, unloved, or "treated like dirt," like "I was nobody," "I was nothing," like "I didn't exist," often by parents in childhood, and then by peers or superiors later in life. The Latin root of the word "humiliation" is *humus*, the word for dirt – a prosaic equivalent of "gilded

---

[1] Gilligan (1996); Gilligan (1999).   [2] Shengold (1989).

loam or painted clay." And the Latin root of the word for extreme humiliation – "mortification" – means "to make dead" (from *mors, mortis*, death, dead; and *facere*, to make). So our language alone tells us that humiliation is a form of "soul murder," or the "death of the self."

These violent prison inmates would say that their insides consisted of straw or other lifeless matter, or that they had ropes or cords inside their bodies instead of nerves or veins. They would cut themselves in order to see the blood flow, to prove to themselves that they were still alive and did have blood inside, and also to see if they could still have feelings, since even pain would be less tormenting than their feeling of numbness and lifelessness. And then they would be surprised and disappointed that even when they inflicted on themselves the most extreme mutilations they still did not experience the sensation of pain, so they would do so repeatedly, not because they felt guilty and were punishing themselves as acts of penance (for they were as incapable of feeling guilt as they were of any other feeling), but in order to see if they could have feelings, which would at least give them the sense of being alive.

The terms they used to describe themselves referred to the living dead: zombies, robots, vampires. One man felt he was a vampire so literally that he killed his grandmother and drank her blood. Some of these men committed the most terrible rapes and murders in order to see if that would enable them to have feelings, and were disappointed to find that even that did not enable them to feel anything at all – neither guilt nor fear of punishment. The common phrase "cold-blooded," as a description of the violent crimes these men committed, is more accurate as a psychological description of these men than most people realize, to refer to those who are as incapable of the warmth of love as they are of the inferno of hate, toward themselves or even toward their victims. They would typically act out their hate toward others, in acts of violence, instead of feeling it.

Some violent men, however, did find that their violence enabled them to have a feeling: not guilt, but pride. That is, they felt proud of having had the "balls" to commit such a violent act. Many of them could not resist the temptation to boast to their friends about what they had done, because they felt it proved what a "real man" they were. (This fact is one thing that makes it easier for the police to discover who committed a violent crime, since all they have to do is to talk to the friends or acquaintances of the suspects.)

These men are often referred to as "shameless," and that is true, but it misses the point: they committed their crime because of the overwhelming shame they had felt prior to doing so, and the commission of the violent acts enabled them to replace the feeling of shame, temporarily, with that of pride. In other words, these men felt neither guilt nor shame for their murders; they felt pride instead – or at least an ersatz substitute for pride, namely, the fear they saw in the eyes of their victims. Only very rarely did these murderers have enough preexisting capacity for guilt feelings to feel guilty about the crime they had just committed. We will discuss those exceptions below, in our analysis of *Othello*.

We speak of shame as a feeling, and indeed it is emotionally painful, but it is really the absence of a feeling: the feeling of love for the self, whether in the form of self-love (pride) or love from others (in the form of honor, reputation, respect, friendship, love, etc.). Perhaps hunger could be seen as analogous: hunger is certainly a painful feeling, but it is caused by the absence of a pleasant and desirable feeling, namely, satiety. Just as hunger is caused by the absence of food in one's body, shame is caused by the absence of love in one's self, whether that is the absence of self-love or love from others.

Some men experienced the death of the self when they had been over-whelmed by shame, and engaged in violence in order to see if they could resurrect their dead self. Others who had not yet been so deeply shamed as to feel that their self had already died committed their violence in order to prevent the death of their self from overwhelming shame.

When people refer to the "instinct of self-preservation," they usually assume that what that refers to is the desire to avoid death, meaning the death of both the body and the mind, which are understood as inextricably coexisting. But what violent men are experiencing, whether in Shakespeare's plays or today's prisons, is the dissociation of the body (the soma) from the self (the psyche). They have decided they prefer death (of the body) to dishonor (which entails the death of the self).

Shame is accompanied by the feeling of innocence, which is also the absence of a feeling: the absence of the feeling of guilt, or self-hate and self-condemnation. So to be overwhelmingly shamed is to not have any feelings invested in the self – neither love nor hate. A self that has no feelings is exactly what these violent men describe themselves as experiencing. We conclude that the self needs love as much as the body needs oxygen, and without love the self dies, just as the body dies when deprived of oxygen. And just as physical pain at least proves to us that we are still alive, so the painful feeling of guilt proves that the self is still alive. Guilt may be painful, but at least it is a feeling (and it is accompanied by the feeling of pride).

What Mowbray and many others in Shakespeare's history plays are referring to, then, when they say that if they lose their honor they lose their life, is neither an exaggeration nor a merely metaphorical way of describing their experience. They are referring to something that is literally true, a psychological fact, that is regularly seen in the most violent men, and the nature of which can be understood in terms of the psychology of shame and guilt. In preferring death to dishonor, they are literally willing to sacrifice their bodies in order to save their souls.

Any illusion that Mowbray is alone in preferring death to dishonor, in feeling that the loss of honor is tantamount to the death of the soul (the self), and that that can be prevented only by means of lethal violence against the person disparaging his honor, is quickly undone by the increasingly adamant statements to the same effect that recur throughout these history plays. Beginning with Mowbray's opponent Bolingbroke, the future Henry IV, and his adversary, Hotspur, this culminates in the uncompromising words and actions of his son, the most honor-crazy and violent of them all, the future Henry V. He loudly and proudly proclaims his choice of an ethical code that prefers honor (the highest value of shame ethics) over the avoidance of sin (the worst evil for guilt ethics): "if it be a sin to covet honor, I am the most offending soul alive" (IV.iii.28–9).

Indeed, Henry V is aware that the values he is living by are those that in the Christian guilt ethic are associated and identified with the devil, and that his notions of "good" are what in that ethic would be called "evil":

> There is some soul of goodness in things evil,
> Would men observingly distill it out;
> For our bad neighbor makes us early stirrers,
> Which is both healthful and good husbandry.
> Besides, they are our outward consciences
> And preachers to us all, admonishing
> That we should dress us fairly for our end.
> Thus may we gather honey from the weed,
> And make a moral of the devil himself.
>
> (IV.i.4–12)

If this were simply an acknowledgment that shame can serve an adaptive, healthy purpose, in stimulating us to wake up and exert ourselves in constructive and healthful (life-protecting) activities, rather than remaining passive, sleeping, and slothful, it would be a psychologically accurate observation. And if it were merely an expression of the need for self-defense, in response to our "bad neighbors" threatening us with violence, that could be seen as a rational, life-protecting exhortation.

But this war was not a defensive war: the French had not declared war against England, nor were they invading England. This war was English aggression against the French. In the context in which it occurs, Henry's speech can only be seen as his attempt to stimulate his troops to be limitlessly violent and destructive, killing as many other people as possible even when that will lead many of his people to their own violent deaths – and all for the sake of honor. And thus it appears to be an embrace of what Milton would later describe as the devil's reversal of the guilt ethic of Christianity into the opposite value system of Lucifer, which we quoted above: "Evil, be thou my good."

It would be hard to imagine a more directly and literally anti-Christian moral sentiment, or a more complete reversal of the guilt ethic of Christianity into the shame ethic of the devil and the "Anti-Christ" (as Nietzsche, in advocating his version of shame ethics, or "Master Morality," would proudly call himself two centuries later). Indeed, it would be hard to find a sentiment more at odds with the guilt ethics of Christianity, such as the Sermon on the Mount, with its absolute prohibition against violence toward others, than in that speech of Henry's.

In case there is any doubt about Henry's value system, and the behavior it commands, we need only notice his address to the citizens of Harfleur, in which Henry's craving for honor and avoiding shame submerges any sense of guilt or remorse. Now fully transformed into a killing machine, he threatens the mass slaughter of all the adults and children in the town (a preview on a smaller scale of what would in later centuries expand into what has come to be called genocide), as well as the mass rape of the enemy's women as a tactic of war (which has been a concomitant of warfare ever since the first documented war, the Trojan War, and has only recently come to be considered a war crime):

> How yet resolves the Governor of the town?
> This is the latest parle we will admit.
> Therefore to our best mercy give yourselves,
> Or like to men proud of destruction
> Defy us to our worst; for, as I am a soldier,
> A name that in my thoughts becomes me best,
> If I begin the battery once again,
> I will not leave the half-achieved Harfleur
> Till in her ashes she lie buried.
> The gates of mercy shall be all shut up,
> And the fleshed soldier, rough and hard of heart,
> In liberty of bloody hand shall range
> With conscience wide as hell, mowing like grass

Your fresh fair virgins and your flowering infants.
What is it then to me if impious way,
Arrayed in flames like to the prince of fiends,
Do with his smirched complexion all fell feats
Enlinked to waste and desolation?
What is't to me, when you yourselves are cause,
If your pure maidens fall in the hand
Of hot and forcing violation?
What rein can hold licentious wickedness
When down the hill he holds his fierce career?
We may as bootless spend our vain command
Upon th'enraged soldiers in their spoil
As send precepts to the leviathan
To come ashore. Therefore, you men of Harfleur,
Take pity of your town and of your people
Whiles yet my soldiers are in my command,
Whiles yet the cool and temperate wind of grace
O'erblows the filthy and contagious clouds
Of heady murder, spoil and villainy.
If not, why, in a moment look to see
The blind and bloody soldier with foul hand
Defile the locks of your shrill-shrieking daughters,
Your fathers taken by their silver beards,
And their most reverend heads dashed to the walls,
Your naked infants spitted upon pikes,
Whiles the mad mothers with their howls confused
Do break the clouds, as did the wives of Jewry
At Herod's bloody-hunting slaughtermen.
What say you? Will you yield and this avoid?
Or, guilty in defence, be thus destroyed?
(Henry V, 3.3.1–43)

Here Henry presses all the stops on the organ of violence:

- He states that he and his men feel proud (not guilty) of the destruction they will cause.
- He proudly proclaims his identity as a soldier (i.e., one whose job it is to kill people) as the best name he can give himself.
- He proclaims that he will burn the entire town to the ground.
- He describes his soldiers as having a "conscience wide as hell," and "arrayed in flames like to the prince of fiends," killing "your fresh fair virgins and your flowering infants" – meaning that they will become the equivalent of the devils in hell, thus reinforcing his identification with the devil and his values, rather than with the opposite values associated with God in heaven.

- He proclaims his complete indifference to all the slaughter, destruction, and cruelty that his decision to go to war will lead to, saying, "What is't to me?," even though he himself states that this slaughter and cruelty are the equivalent of the values and behavior of the devil, "the prince of fiends," concerning which he feels completely innocent (not guilty) himself.

And in case there was any doubt about how completely innocent he feels for all the devastation he is threatening to inflict on the citizens of Harfleur, he winds up blaming the victims rather than himself for the violence he threatens them with, including the mass rapes of their daughters. For, as he puts it, it is the citizens of Harfleur who will be guilty for all this: "guilty in defence." In other words, guilty for attempting to defend themselves and their families from his aggression. And he says this after already having admitted (without feeling any guilt over it) that the actions he is threatening them with are "licentious wickedness," "the filthy and contagious clouds / Of heady murder, spoil and villainy," committed with "foul hand," and so on. He describes this limitless, absolutely uninhibited cruelty and violence with no sense of guilt whatsoever, but rather, as a source of honor and pride. "Evil be thou my good" indeed!

Henry V's actions here are what we now call "war crimes" and "crimes against humanity." Slightly extended, they would be called genocide. But Henry V is far from being the only character in this play who reveals the power of shame to motivate people not only to want to kill others in order to gain or maintain their honor but also to prefer their own deaths to dishonor, when that is the price they need to pay for honor. For example, when the French Dauphin realizes his army is defeated and retreating, he cries, "Reproach and everlasting shame Sits mocking in our plumes.... Do not run away." Then the Constable exclaims: "Why, all our ranks are broke." To which the Dauphin replies: "O perdurable shame! Let's stab ourselves." And the Duke of Bourbon cries:

> Shame and eternal shame, nothing but shame!
> Let us die! In once more! Back again!
> And he that will not follow Bourbon now
> Let him go hence, and with his cap in hand
> Like a base pander hold the chamber-door
> Whilst [by a] slave, no gentler than a dog
> His fairest daughter is contaminated. (10–16)
> CONSTABLE: Let us on heaps go offer up our lives. (18)
> BOURBON: Let life be short, else shame will be too long. (23)
> (IV.v.4–23)

It is crucial here to remember that we believe Shakespeare is best understood as a psychologist who is showing us how and why people do behave, and the consequences thereof, not a moralist preaching to us as to how they should behave. The plays we are discussing here are not "morality plays," they are history plays. And in them Shakespeare shows what the people he is bringing to life on the stage are thinking and feeling and doing, and leaves it up to us to make up our own minds as to how we would understand and evaluate them.

Given that, we think it is a sign of his sheer genius to have invented such a remarkable contrast to Prince Hal/Henry V as Falstaff. For in Falstaff we have the picture of a man who is virtually impervious to the emotions of both shame and guilt. It is through the contrast between Falstaff and the major protagonists of the history plays that Shakespeare shines a spotlight on the psychology of shame and guilt – in this case by showing what their absence would look like. From a moral standpoint, we would describe Falstaff as an "amoral hedonist," by which we mean that he never developed either a shame ethic or a guilt ethic.

In the midst of the ongoing civil war against Henry IV, Falstaff, recruited to fight alongside Hal on the king's side, eschews participation and explains why in his great speech on honor:

PRINCE: Why, thou owest God a death.   *[Exit.]*
FALSTAFF: 'Tis not due yet. I would be loath to pay him before his day. What need I be so forward with him that calls not on me? Well, 'tis no matter; honour pricks on. Yes, but how if honour prick me off when I come on? Can honour set to a leg? No. Or an arm? No. Or take away the grief of a wound? No. Honour hath no skill in surgery, then? No. What is honour? A word. What is in that word 'honour'? What is that 'honour'? Air. Who hath it? He that died o' Wednesday. Doth he feel it? No. Doth he hear it? No. 'Tis insensible, then? Yea, to the dead. But will it not live with the living? No. Why? Detraction will not suffer it. There I'll none of it. Honour is a mere scutcheon. And so ends my catechism.... (*1 Henry IV*, 5.1.126–40)

In this respect, Falstaff is like a child who has not yet developed a capacity for feelings of either shame or guilt. Or to put it in mythological terms, like Adam in the Garden of Eden before he ate the fruit of the tree of the knowledge of good and evil and became sensitive to the first moral emotion, namely, shame. For Falstaff approaches the world as if it were the Garden of Eden, in which if you are hungry, you merely pick the lowest-lying fruit from the nearest tree; but you certainly never behave like Cain, whose behavior shows what can happen when people have developed a sense of shame.

We have no desire to idealize Falstaff, or to ignore his many limitations, in comparison with human beings who have the potential for intellectual and artistic creativity, as well as for taking care of those who need help and compassion. Whatever he is, he is no saint, no genius, and no hero. The cost of his shamelessness – the fact that he seems never to have developed a sense of shame or a sensitivity to that painful emotion – is revealed by his failure to have any apparent need for achievement or the full development of whatever potentialities he was born with (except, of course, for eating and drinking). And he remains dependent on others to take care of him and provide what he needs, though his needs are simple and easily met. He specifically does not "work for a living." On the other hand, a benefit of his shamelessness is that he also does not seem to hate anyone, or to have any particular wish to commit violence, or inflict any serious injuries, on anyone – himself or anyone else. In comparison with Henry V, he is remarkably harmless.

Given the absence of shame, he does not experience feelings of hate or impulses toward violence, so he does not need a capacity for, or sensitivity to, feelings of guilt. But his lack of a guilt-sensitive conscience does manifest itself in his willingness to commit property crimes (as opposed to violent crimes, i.e., injuring or killing people); he merely wants their money, not their lives. Like a little child, he acts as if the world owes him a living – but unlike Henry V, he is perfectly happy to let everyone else go on living. So he does show the behavioral limitations of the imperviousness to guilt, a kind of limited sociopathy, but nothing remotely comparable to the viciousness and murderousness and deliberate cruelty of his old pal, now Henry V.

Indeed, he pays the cost of his failure to develop more of an ability to take care of himself when he is shunned by Henry and loses the will to live. But that could be attributed also to his simple, uncomplicated, and quite spontaneous affection for Prince Hal, whose failure to return that friendship was literally deadly for this man. In fact, Falstaff seems to have become capable only of playing, not working, so that his friendship with Prince Hal has more of the quality of being playmates, like children, rather than adult friends who have a genuine attachment to each other and also a capacity to function independently of the other when necessary. Or we could suggest that when Henry was Prince Hal, a late adolescent, Falstaff was a kind of undemanding, unchallenging, and even in some ways nurturing father to him, but that when Prince Hal became Henry V and rejected him, Falstaff was more like a child abandoned by his father – or an elderly, disabled father abandoned by his adult son.

But the major implication we wish to draw our readers' attention to is the extreme brilliance of Falstaff's (meaning Shakespeare's) revelation of the inanity and destructiveness that the very concepts of shame and honor, and of the moral, cultural, and political value systems associated with them, can have.

At the same time, Henry V (the former Prince Hal) also demonstrates the utter inability of shame-driven personalities to understand the motives and values of those who are indifferent to shame. What's more, he also shows us the tone-deafness of shame-driven personalities to those who are sensitive to shame but who have repudiated shame-motivated values and behaviors because they also have an internalized conscience and are capable of guilt feelings. The opposite is also true: the guilt-ridden tend to find the motives and behaviors of the shame-driven incomprehensible and shocking. So the incomprehension is often mutual. The guilt-ridden often make the mistake of thinking that those who are shame-driven are simply immoral or amoral (with no moral value system), rather than realizing that they in fact have a very real value system – it just happens to be the opposite of their own.

Falstaff continues his deconstruction of honor when he remarks, "Give me life, which if I can save, so; if not, honour comes unlook'd for, and there's an end." But in any case, he makes it clear that given the choice, he would always choose life over "honor." He does the same thing again when he pretends to be dead because of his fear that Hotspur will kill him, until Henry kills Hotspur. He then gets off the ground, and reflects that

> Sblood, 'twas time to counterfeit [being dead], or that hot termagant Scot had paid me scot and lot too. Counterfeit? I lie, I am no counterfeit. To die is to be a counterfeit, for he is but the counterfeit of a man who hath not the life of a man; but to counterfeit dying, when a man thereby liveth, is to be no counterfeit, but the true and perfect image of life indeed. The better part of valor is discretion, in the which better part I have saved my life.
> (*1 Henry IV*, V.iv.113–21)

In short, in comparison with the murderous Henry V, Falstaff appears to be the very model of mental health (as it would appear in a child or young adolescent – meaning the capacity to remain alive and be a nonviolent playmate). But what he shows is not the inhibition of violence by guilt-sensitive ethics and politics. Rather, he embodies the replacement of both moral emotions, shame and guilt, with the emotion that transcends them both – namely, the perfectly natural and healthy emotions of self-love, coupled with love toward others (or at least the absence of hate, and the capacity for a childlike friendship with an adult playmate). Thus, he seeks to gain pleasure for himself, even if that means helping himself to other people's change-purses, but not at the expense of physical violence against others.

And as we said just above, while his relative absence of sensitivity to shame means that he is not motivated to achieve culturally valuable accomplishments, at least he is relatively harmless, which is more than can be said for most of the chief protagonists in the history plays and the tragedies (and in much of human history). One might say of him that he does obey the first rule of medicine: *primum non nocere*: first of all, do no harm. And while it is true that the more or less complete immunity to shame of the Falstaffs of this world means that they are unlikely to fulfill the additional tasks of medical experts – far be it from a Falstaff to have sufficient need for achievement to develop the "miracles" of modern medicine – at least they do not create more work for the trauma surgeons, let alone the undertakers. But it does not appear to be a strict conscience or intense guilt feelings that inhibit Falstaff from being violent toward others. In addition to being free from the powerful stimulant to violence that shame is, he also has a combination of prudent awareness that violence against others would provoke them to violence against him, which his self-love alone motivates him to avoid.[3]

It is in the creation of Falstaff, and the description of his relationship with Prince Hal/Henry V, that Shakespeare illuminates an important paradox: namely, that even when the absurdity and destructiveness of the value systems of shame ethics and shame cultures are demonstrated and ridiculed, that demonstration alone has no effect on shame-driven personalities and cultures. The shame-driven Henry V cannot even hear or understand how anyone could disagree with his belief that the pursuit of honor and the avoidance of shame are the most important and legitimate values that should guide his behavior. And this is true despite the fact that those values often motivate virtually limitless violence toward others, and risk causing the death of the self as well. At no point does Prince Hal/Henry V attempt to refute Falstaff's demolition of honor. Shakespeare leaves it as an open question as to whether or not Henry has the emotional and cognitive capacity even to understand Falstaff's humane skepticism about honor as a value worth killing and dying for. In any case, Henry V certainly shows no evidence of having any incentive

[3] See, for a celebration of Falstaff's patriarchally unscripted free humanity, Bloom (1998), pp. 271–314.

to question his own assumption that honor is the supreme value, or any apparent awareness that it could be questioned by anyone worth listening to.

The obverse is also true: there is no way that Falstaff could entertain for one second the possibility that Henry's values and ethos make any sense. For Falstaff it is simply self-evident, a matter of common sense, that life is more valuable than so-called honor. The two of them simply talk past one another, with neither one understanding the other, or why the other thinks and behaves as he does. They simply fail to communicate.

Ironically, we see anticipated in Shakespeare's history plays two of Jean Piaget's findings, from his studies of cognitive development in young children. For example, a very young child may just take it as self-evident that when he places a pencil in a glass of water, the pencil ruptures – it divides into two parts – but then recomposes itself when he takes it out of the water: for he can see that happen with his own eyes, and even for that young a child, observation is taken as an independent source of knowledge. Yet an older child realizes that the apparent division of the pencil in water is merely an optical illusion, and that the physical integrity of the pencil is constant, not shape-shifting.

The relevance of this to Falstaff and Henry is two-fold: people at an earlier stage of cognitive development simply do not have the cognitive capacity to understand the world as those at a later stage of development do. But it is also true that once people advance from an earlier to a later stage, they tend to forget that they ever thought the way they did when they were younger. That is, they think that since the way they think now is obviously true, it must have always been true, and they cannot understand how anyone could ever have thought that pencils divide themselves when placed in water, and that therefore they must always have known that pencils do not behave in that way.

So not only does Henry not understand what Falstaff is saying; Falstaff cannot understand why Henry would think and feel (and therefore act) as he does. And in fact, this failure of each of them to understand the other finally results in the rupture of their relationship – which we, at least as readers and spectators of these plays, feel was a loss for both of them. (Certainly, Falstaff thought it was.)

But more importantly, this same failure runs throughout the history of moral, legal, and political thought. For example, in contemporary America, millions of people continue to idolize our recent right-wing president (Trump) and simply cannot understand why his opponents see him as narcissistic, sociopathic, and violence-provoking (what we are calling shame-driven), nor even why he has any opponents; and since they cannot see any rational reasons for opposing their hero, they resort to demonizing the president's opponents, and even subjecting them to violence. However, those who see that former president as a violence-provoking would-be tyrant who would undermine democracy and the rule of law, and who is guilty of serious crimes, find it difficult to understand how anyone could see him differently from the way they do, and how he could even have supporters at all. So what we have is an almost complete breakdown of communication and understanding between the two sides, which is, potentially, very dangerous, not only for America but for the whole world. This pattern, of course, does not occur only in this country, with this president, and in this century.

Are there any solutions for this problem of mutual misunderstanding and incomprehension? This book is not the place for any extensive attempts to answer such a question. Nor do we pretend to have any complete or definitive answers. What we will suggest, however, as at least the first step toward a solution, is what both Shakespeare and Piaget, and the whole tradition of psychoanalytic and psychological research have provided us with, each in their own way: namely, psychological understanding of the strengths and limitations of both points of view, in this case, the shame-driven and the guilt-sensitive, in personality as well as in culture.

For what Shakespeare shows us is a repeated series of examples of the two "equal and opposite" moral and political value systems, as they operate in people's lives (though more often, of the shame-driven, as those are both more common and more dangerous than are those of the guilt-sensitive). But by placing a shame-driven character side by side with one who is not, that is, Henry with Falstaff, Shakespeare makes it possible to gain a much clearer psychological understanding of shame ethics and the difficulty of transcending shame ethics, even when its core value of honor has been exposed as life-threatening. One might say that what Henry V needed was guilt ethics, but that lies outside the bounds of this play.

Where guilt ethics enters the history plays is with Henry VI. In his three plays about the only son and heir of Henry V, Shakespeare brings to life a character radically different from both Falstaff and Henry V, though he has more in common with the former than with the latter. The son is as gentle as his father was fierce, as humble as his father was proud, as forgiving as his father was vengeful, as dedicated to making peace as his father was to making war, and (like Falstaff) as disdainful of the conventional notion of "honor" as Henry was a slave to it. And given the discrepancy between the demands

made on heirs to the throne at the time at which he lived, he as much as
Hamlet was a victim of the fact that, for him, the time was indeed out of
joint: he was born before his time, that is, before a person such as him could
survive the shark-infested political waters into which he was cast.

The politics of that time are described by Lord Exeter, who notes the
violence-breeding nature of envy (a variety of shame):

> No simple man that sees
> This jarring discord of nobility
> This shouldering of each other in the court,
> This factious bandying of their favorites,
> But that it doth presage some ill event.
> 'Tis much, when scepters are in children's hands:
> But more, when envy breeds unkind division,
> There comes the ruin, there begins confusion.
>
> (*1 Henry VI*, IV.i.193–4)

One could hardly ask for a more searing indictment of the political
system called monarchy and oligarchy, or aristocracy and autocracy. What
Shakespeare experienced and observed firsthand was a political system
whose centuries of virtually unlimited violence and cruelty, revenge and
counterrevenge, he then dramatized in the most exquisite detail.

As Henry VI describes himself, "No sooner was I crept out of my cradle /
But I was made a king, at nine months old. Was never subject long'd to be a
king As I do long and wish to be a subject" (*2 Henry VI*, IV.ix.3–6) – a
sentiment of humility that he repeats at length and repeatedly throughout
the three plays. He is thus as exact an example of a guilt-ridden, or guilt-
sensitive, personality as any that Shakespeare brought to life before he
created Othello and Hamlet. And he exemplifies both the strengths and
the weaknesses of that character structure.

It would hardly be an exaggeration to say that Henry VI was as close to
being a Christ-figure as anyone could be who was also king of England at
that time, and that as a result he suffered a fate not as cruel, but just as
deadly, as that of Christ – he was murdered. This is not to say that he was a
saint. As king, he did submit to the law of the time in condemning to
death some who were guilty of breaking the law. And yet he went out of
his way to pardon thousands of others, and to repudiate revenge as an
acceptable response, when it was a matter of his choice, not the law's.

The first description of Henry, in the three plays devoted to him, is
Gloucester's characterization of him as "an effeminate prince, Whom like a
schoolboy you may overawe" (*1 Henry VI*, I.i.35–6). And as soon as he had

reached puberty, and his courtiers were seeking to find an acceptable queen for him, he stated, with a remarkable combination of innocence, naivete, and piety, "Marriage, uncle! Alas, my years are young! / And fitter is my study and my books / Than wanton dalliance with a paramour" (*1 Henry VI*, V.i.21–3). For he himself is more pious than many of the politically ambitious churchmen of his time. When he realizes that he will be given a great gift (a beautiful wife), he responds not with a sense of entitlement, but of gratitude to God:

> O Lord, that lends me life,
> Lend me a heart replete with thankfulness!
> For thou hast given me in this beauteous face
> A world of earthly blessings to my soul.
> (*2 Henry VI*, I.i.19–22)

His most notable characteristic, however, is his desire to be a peace-maker, rather than a warmonger. When his chief ministers are beginning to quarrel with each other, he says (in language reminiscent of Falstaff's and Hamlet's):

> Good Lord, what madness rules in brainsick men,
> When for so slight and frivolous a cause
> Such factious emulations shall arise!
> Good cousins both, of York and Somerset,
> Quiet yourselves, I pray, and be at peace.
> (*1 Henry VI*, IV.i.111–15)

And "as we hither came in peace, / So let us still continue peace, and love" (*1 Henry VI*, IV.i.160–1).

Early on, he describes the hypocrisy he observed himself surrounded by, when he states that

> I always thought
> It was both impious and unnatural
> That such immunity and bloody strife
> Should reign among professors of one faith [i.e., Christianity].
> (*1 Henry VI*, V.i.11–14)

As a peacemaker, he references the Beatitudes from the Sermon on the Mount, reinforcing the association of him with Christ, as if Shakespeare were saying to us: don't miss the point here:

> I prithee peace,
> Good queen, and whet not on these furious peers,
> For blessed are the peacemakers on earth.
> (*2 Henry VI*, II.i.33–35)

And in anticipation of the references to the Sermon on the Mount that Shakespeare again alludes to in *Measure for Measure*, Henry says, after Gloucester's murder:

> O Thou that judgest all things, stay my thoughts;
> Some violent hands were laid on Humphrey's life!
> If my suspect be false, forgive me God,
> For judgment only doth belong to thee.
>
> (*2 Henry VI*, III.ii.137–40)

When Buckingham calls upon him to decide how to deal with the rebels who have followed Jack Cade in seeking to overthrow and potentially kill him, asking, "What answer makes your Grace to rebels' supplication?" Henry answers:

> I'll send some holy bishop to entreat;
> For God forbid so many simple souls
> Should perish by the sword! And I myself,
> Rather than bloody war shall cut them short,
> Will parley with Jack Cade their general.
>
> (*2 Henry VI*, IV.iv.7–12)

Repeatedly, Henry VI chooses not to resort to violence or revenge, and to rely on words rather than force as the way to respond to a potentially life-threatening attempt at revolution (the rough equivalent to which actually did result, in a later century, in the beheading of his seventeenth-century successor in the monarchy, Charles I).

When he observes that another person, Richard Plantagenet, who has attempted to overthrow and even kill him, has been beheaded, he again renounces violent revenge as an acceptable response, and protests his innocence: he doesn't endorse this terrible crime, he disavows this deed of violence. Seeing Richard's head, he says: "To see this sight, it irks my very soul. Withhold revenge, dear God! 'tis not my fault" (*3 Henry VI*, II.ii.6–7)

Not surprisingly, given that Shakespeare was describing the relatively pure and extreme shame culture that existed at the time he was writing about, many of Henry's companions were appalled and shamed by his guilt ethic moral values. For example, no sooner had he uttered his disavowal of the moral propriety of beheading his political rival, Richard of York, than his courtier Clifford exclaimed:

> this too much lenity
> And harmful pity must be put aside.
>
> (*2 Henry VI*, II.ii.9–10)

More strongly, Clifford shames Henry for preferring peace and non-violence to the preservation of his own dynasty, when Henry offers to let

Edward rather than his own son inherit the kingship: "For shame, my liege ... what a shame were this!" (*3 Henry VI*, II.ii.6–10). To which Henry replies (in the true Christian spirit): "I'll leave my son my virtuous deeds behind, and would my father had left me no more!" (II.ii.45–8).

Even Henry's Queen shames him for his nonviolence: "What are you made of? You'll nor fight nor fly" (*2 Henry VI*, V.ii.74). And regarding his agreement to let Edward inherit his throne, she says how ashamed she is of him, that he prefers life to honor, and for which she is divorcing him:

> Art thou king, and wilt be forc'd?
> I shame to hear thee speak. Ah, timorous wretch ...
> Such safety finds
> The trembling lamb environed with wolves.
> ... thou prefer'st thy life before thine honor;
> And seeing thou dost, I here divorce myself
> From thy table, Henry, and thy bed ...
> ... thy foul disgrace.
>
> (*3 Henry VI*, I.i.229–53)

Indeed, virtually all his courtiers express how shameful they feel he is to prefer peace and nonviolence to continued war with Edward, in terms including "Base, fearful and despairing Henry! ... How hast thou injur'd both thyself and us! ... faint-hearted and degenerate king, / In whose cold blood no spark of honor bides ... die in bands for this unmanly deed! ... live in peace abandon'd and despised" (*3 Henry VI*, I.i.177–88).

Nevertheless, Henry VI goes on to pursue peace, nonviolence, and what today would be called "conflict resolution," when he says "friendly counsel cuts off many foes" (*3 Henry VI*, III.i.185).

Shakespeare went far out of his way to identify Henry VI as a kind of Christ-figure (i.e., a person committed to the principles of love and forgiveness). In order to make sure we do not miss that point, Shakespeare has Henry paraphrase not once but three times the forgiveness and understanding that Jesus expressed toward those who were crucifying him, saying, "Father, forgive them, for they know not what they do" (Luke 23:34). When Henry is captured by a game-keeper, whom he knows is in the service of his opponent Edward Plantagenet, who has stolen his throne and could reasonably be expected to imprison or even kill him, he says:

> Ah, simple men, you know not what you swear! ...
> What God will, that let your king perform,
> And what he will, I humbly yield unto.
>
> (*3 Henry VI*, III.i.83, 100–1)

This expresses not only his refusal to hold them accountable for their violence against him but also his pursuit and acceptance of humility and nonviolence, rather than of pride, dominance, and superiority.

And then again, after he has regained the throne, and has just had to suppress the rebellion led by Jack Cade, he forgives the rebels, whom he knows are among the most powerless and impoverished members of his kingdom, saying, "O graceless men! They know not what they do" (2 *Henry VI*, IV.iv.38) – thus literally quoting one of the "Seven Last Words" of Christ on the cross.

And in his final act of forgiving those who were committing violence against him, he says to God, and to Richard of York (the future Richard III), who is stabbing him to death: "O God forgive my sins, and pardon thee!" (3 *Henry VI*, V.vi.60). These prove to be his last words, in which, like Jesus, he prays to God to forgive the man who is murdering him.

Shakespeare thus shows how deadly the political system of monarchy was for someone who actually lived according to the highest and most sacred values that this Christian society professed to believe in. And if there were any doubts about the deadliness of this hierarchical, shame-driven, political system for everyone involved, Richard III dispels them.

For Shakespeare's most remarkable portrait of the psychological roots of psychopathic violence in a shame-driven personality is Richard III. Richard's humiliation, and the degree to which he was deprived of love from childhood to adulthood, is shown in the play with great care, prefiguring many variations on the same general theme in the later tragedies. Richard's opening speech in the play is a detailed inventory of all the motives for his conscious intention to kill others without any inhibitions or guilt feelings in order to get revenge on nature and humanity for the overwhelming shame and humiliation he feels over having a "hunchback," which he concludes has made him unattractive and unlovable, as a man, to all women. Referring to the deformity of his back, and why it was leading him to continue his own private war even after peace has come to England, he says:

> Grim-visaged War hath smoothed his wrinkled front:
> And now, instead of mounting barbed steeds
> To fright the souls of fearful adversaries,
> He capers nimbly in a lady's chamber
> To the lascivious pleasing of a lute.
> But I, that am not shaped for sportive tricks,
> Nor made to court an amorous looking-glass;

> I, that am rudely stamped, and want love's majesty
> To strut before a wanton ambling nymph;
> I, that am curtailed of this fair proportion,
> Cheated of feature by dissembling nature,
> Deformed, unfinished, sent before my time
> Into this breathing world, scarce half made up,
> And that so lamely and unfashionable
> That dogs bark at me as I halt by them –
> Why, I, in this weak piping time of peace,
> Have no delight to pass away the time,
> Unless to see my shadow in the sun
> And descant on mine own deformity.
> And therefore, since I cannot prove a lover
> To entertain these fair well-spoken days,
> I am determined to prove a villain . . .
> Plots have I laid, . . .
> And if King Edward be as true and just
> As I am subtle, false, and treacherous . . .
>
> (*Richard III*, I.2.9–37)

Richard's detailed recitation of how his deformity provoked shame, rage, and violence is not merely a string of isolated or random associations. Shakespeare provides us here with a brilliant illustration of what research on the psychology of murder today affirms.

For example, a young man in his twenties, interviewed in connection with his murder trial in Omaha, Nebraska, had attempted to revenge himself on an ex-fiancée who had rejected him, by committing the "perfect crime." He worked in a cancer research laboratory, so he had access to a carcinogenic chemical, which he placed in the lemonade in her refrigerator, so that she would develop cancer at a later date and murder would never be suspected. As it turned out, she never drank the contaminated liquids, but several others did and two died soon thereafter; since he had placed so much of the chemical in the liquids, they died from the immediate toxic effect rather than from the long-term carcinogenic one. Prior to committing this self-consciously "diabolical" crime, he had become obsessed with the literature of a cult that engaged in devil-worship and "black masses." That is, he consciously placed a positive value on identifying with the devil and being "evil," as that moral value is defined in terms of Judeo-Christian ethics, just as Richard consciously resolves to "prove a villain" and be "subtle, false and treacherous." The young man in Omaha was found guilty of murder and sentenced to death – a punishment which is also a direct repudiation of the guilt ethic that Jesus preached.

Berton Roueche devoted one of his "Annals of Medicine" articles in *The New Yorker* to this modern incarnation of Richard III, although Roueche's focus was on how the Omaha police discovered "who dunnit," that is, who had committed the murder.[4] What interests us here is the question one of us, Gilligan, explored in interviewing this man in preparation for his trial, namely, *why* had he "dunit"? and it was here that the analogy to Richard III became clear.

In his childhood, this man had suffered a "loss of face" in an even more painful and literal sense than that phrase usually connotes: a gasoline can he was playing with as a child had exploded in his face, burning off the skin and (literally) "effacing" him with scars which years of plastic surgery had not been able to undo completely. The parallel with Richard could not have been more exact: the man was so deeply humiliated and shamed by his physical deformity that he felt he was not lovable and could not be loved by any woman, so he resolved consciously to become a villain and identified with the devil and the devil's values.

In *Richard III*, we learn from his own mother, the Duchess of York, how she feels about this son:

> by the Holy Rood, though knowest it well:
> Thou cam'st on earth to make the earth my hell.
> A grievous burden was thy birth to me;
> Tetchy and way ward was thy infancy.
> Thy school days frightful, desperate, wild and furious;
> Thy primes of manhood daring, bold and venturous;
> Thy age confirmed proud, subtle, sly and bloody,
> More mild, but yet more harmful, kind in hatred.
> What comfortable hour canst thou name
> That ever graced me with thy company?
>
> (*Richard III*, IV.iv.166–75)

Thus Shakespeare describes with pitch-perfect accuracy what today is understood as the recipe for creating a violent, psychopathic personality: raise someone without love, which is another way of saying, shame them from their childhood on. This sets up a perfect vicious cycle: the more unloved they are, the more they will behave in ways that make them even more unlovable. Thus it is hardly surprising that Richard would grow up to become hypersensitive to shame, and incapable of feelings of guilt over even the cruelest behavior toward others.[5]

---

[4] Roueche (1982).
[5] For Freud on this point, citing this speech in *Richard III*, see Freud (1957), pp. 314–15.

We do not need to itemize all of the instances of Richard's manipulations and betrayals of virtually everyone with whom he interacts in order to advance his quest for power and prestige – or in other words, for narcissistic gratifications with which to heal his narcissistic wounds – and for revenge against the whole world for having exposed him to a lifelong source of shame and humiliation. He has clearly summarized his motives for this behavior in the soliloquy with which he opens the play. The main thing we have to add to this is an example of how closely Shakespeare mirrors in this play and this character exactly what we see today, not on the stage, or in a fantasied reconstruction of an historical figure, but in real, observable life (and death).

At the end of the play, before the final battle in which he will be killed, Richard experiences in dreams a succession of the various people whom he has killed in the course of the play's action, who he knows would condemn him for his wrongdoing, as well as a conscious awareness of how completely he had violated the guilt ethic that coexisted in his culture with the shame ethic that he himself had obeyed, and an awareness that his doing so had resulted in his own complete ruination – about all of which, he is clearly conflicted and tossed back and forth into a confused mixture of contrarieties:

> Give me another horse! Bind up my wounds!
> Have mercy, Jesu – Soft, I did but dream.
> O coward conscience, how dost thou afflict me!
> The lights burn blue. It is now dead midnight.
> Cold fearful drops stand on my trembling flesh.
> What do I fear? Myself? There's none else by.
> Richard loves Richard, that is, I am I.
> Is there a murderer here? No. Yes, I am.
> Then fly! What, from myself? Great reason why?
> Lest I revenge. What, myself upon myself?
> Alack, I love myself. Wherefore? For any good
> That I myself have done myself?
> O, no. Alas, I rather hate myself,
> For hateful deeds committed by myself.
> I am a villain. Yet I lie, I am not.
> Fool, of thyself speak well. Fool, do not flatter.
> My conscience hath a thousand several tongues,
> And every tongue condemns me for a villain.
> Perjury, perjury, in the highest degree;
> All several sins, all used in such degree,
> Throng to the bar, crying all, "Guilty, guilty!"
> I shall despair. There is no creature loves me
> And wherefore should they, since that I myself

Find in myself no pity to myself?
Methought the souls of all that I had murdered
Came to my tent, and every one did threat
Tomorrow's vengeance on the head of Richard.
(*Richard III*, V.iii.177–206)

Richard understands perfectly well that all others, including his victims, condemn him for his murders and seek retribution. He seems to think that he should feel guilty because everyone else condemns him, but he has no space in his psyche for conscience, which he sees only as causing cowardice. He hears from the "thousand several tongues" of his conscience that he is guilty of murder. But since he believes his conscience is also the voice of cowardice (nonviolence) and therefore of shame, and he knows of no alternative to murder as the means for attaining pride and undoing his shame, he rejects and repudiates the voice of his conscience and is unable to integrate it into his personality. He knows that if he listened to his conscience, he would hate himself and call himself a villain, and take revenge on himself, or punish himself, for the lethal violence he has inflicted on others. But he immediately rejects that moral judgment.

He experiences his conscience as an internalized voice that he hears, argues with, and ultimately repudiates. That internalized voice condemns him as a villain, and says he should feel guilty and hate himself for the heinous deeds he has committed. But he rejects the guilt ethics that he hears his conscience advocating on the grounds that he would be a fool if he did not speak well of himself.

Thus Richard III is not able to abandon the central principle of the shame ethic that has guided his behavior throughout his murderous career – namely, that it is better to be a knave (i.e., a villain) than a fool – because that moral value system has shown him the only way he knows by which to escape shame and achieve pride. So, if he obeyed the commands of his conscience and condemned, hated, and punished himself, he would be both a coward and a fool – two of the most shameful identities there are. Better to be a villain than a coward and a fool! So Richard rejects guilt and self-hate.

But this does not solve his dilemma, which is that his violent behavior pattern, although its whole purpose was to enable him to gain more love of himself, has not enabled him to achieve any stable self-love either. And it has only provoked hate, not love, from others. What makes this touching, even moving, is that he acknowledges both the cause and the consequence of his psychopathic personality and behavior when he says, "No creature loves me."

Richard III cannot accept guilt ethics, but shame ethics has not worked for him either. So he reaches a state of despair, being forced to recognize that his whole strategy for living and achieving self-esteem, by pursuing a shame ethic, has been a colossal failure.

What he has discovered can be seen repeatedly in violent men: namely, turning to violence and revenge, as attempts to satisfy the thirst for self-love and love from others when one has received only hate and contempt from others and is tormented by self-contempt, is like drinking salt water in order to quench one's thirst. One may think that will do the trick, at first, but then it turns out only to exacerbate the problem. So Richard finds in himself "no pity to myself" or, in other words, no love, or even compassion, for himself, but an emotional vacancy instead – neither self-love nor love from others.[6] No wonder he reaches a state of despair.

We close our discussion of the history plays by reiterating our observation that despite the extent to which these plays, and *Henry V* especially, have often been read by taking at face value the prizing of honor, the call to battle, and the glory of war as in Henry's famous St. Crispin's Day speech ("We few, we happy few, we band of brothers / For he today that sheds his blood with me shall be my brother" – IV.iii.60–1), the text itself could not be more clear in exposing the underside of this shame/honor ethic. One has only to note the chorus that Shakespeare appends as an epilogue to Henry V, reminding the audience that Henry died very young, leaving the kingdom to his infant son, during whose reign France was lost and England did "bleed."

In a footnote, the editor of *Henry V in* the *Riverside Shakespeare* comments that the royal wedding at the end of the play did not bring the predicted peace and the achievement of Henry's goals, "for the Dauphin, indignant at the concessions that Henry had exacted from his father, continued his resistance. Consequently, Henry's last two years of life were spent in an unsuccessful effort to consolidate his gains in France. When he died in 1422, leaving the throne to his infant son, affairs were in the disordered state described at the opening of *1 Henry VI*."[7] Any impression that the political system and the culture of shame and honor described in these history plays succeeded in finding ways for people to resolve their conflicts and live in peace with one another is belied by these reminders that the reality was an unending cycle not only of wars with neighboring kingdoms (France) but of civil wars within the kingdom of England itself.

---

[6] We are indebted for this point to our student, Michael Lessard.   [7] Baker (1974), p. 971.

In saying this, we would be remiss to overlook another point explicitly made by these history plays, specifically with reference to the peace-loving Henry VI. We have noted his guilt ethic, his embodiment of Christ's example of valuing forgiveness and refusing violence, and his repeated allusions to and endorsement of the ethics of the Sermon on the Mount. With these examples of his guilt-driven, war-abjuring character, we have also included the references to him by other characters in the play (virtually all his courtiers) as "unmanly," "effeminate," and "fearful," as "This faint-hearted and degenerate king in whose cold blood no spark of honor bides." Henry's peace-loving nature, his questioning of a shame ethic, and his refusal to embrace honor as the highest value thus become grounds for questioning his masculinity, his manhood.

In different ways we have written about the affinity between a shame ethic and the culture and the politics of patriarchy. In *Violence: Reflections on a National Epidemic*, I (James Gilligan), wrote about the making of manhood and the violence of men. Male gender codes teach boys and men to acquiesce in a "code of honor" that exposes them to physical injury, pain, and death and requires them to inflict those injuries on other men and sometimes on women as well. The patriarchal structure around which shame cultures are organized becomes apparent when we notice that "men and women stand in a markedly different relationship to the whole system of allotting honor. In 'cultures of honor' . . . it is men and only men "who are expected to be violent and who are honored for doing so and who are dishonored for being unwilling to be violent."[8]

In *Disarming Manhood: Roots of Ethical Resistance*, I (David Richards) studied men who abjured violence.[9] William Lloyd Garrison, Mohandas Gandhi, and Martin Luther King Jr., among others, shared an alternative psychology, springing from a religious outlook that enabled them to resist traditional male responses to challenges, including assaults on their manhood. Like Henry VI, many appealed to the ethics of the Sermon on the Mount. In *Boys' Secrets and Men's Loves*, the point is extended to show how deeply patriarchy harms men, both those who endorse its codes of honor and those who refuse to live according to them.

---

[8] Gilligan (1997), pp. 230–1.   [9] Richards (2005).

CHAPTER 3

Fathers and Mothers
The Perversion of Love in King Lear and Coriolanus

In the opening lines of *King Lear*, the Earl of Kent asks the Earl of Gloucester if Edmund, who is present, is his son. Gloucester in reply does not just acknowledge that he is. He adds that he is ashamed of having such a son: "His breeding, sir, hath been at my charge. I have so often blush'd" (i.e., been ashamed) "to acknowledge him, that now I am braz'd" (brazened, or hardened) "to't" (I.1.9–11). He refers to Edmund as a "knave," but "the whoreson must be acknowledg'd."

To his father, Edmund is a knave and the son of a "whore." And while this term might not express as much overt hostility as the modern version, "son of a bitch," it nevertheless makes it clear that Edmund is a bastard, his mother a whore, and therefore there is something shameful about the status of both Edmund and his mother: shameful not only to them but also to Gloucester. His paternity, he says, "*must* be acknowledg'd" (emphasis added), not that he happily and voluntarily does so. And Edmund's shameful or inferior status is confirmed by the legal and economic status system of the time, which on the grounds of his illegitimacy withholds full recognition of his parentage and inheritance, granting them only to his half-brother Edgar, Gloucester's "legitimate" son.

Let us think for a moment about Gloucester's describing Edmund as both a "knave" and a "whoreson." Frank Kermode[1] states that "knave" merely means "young fellow (not derogatory)," and Onions' *Shakespeare Glossary*[2] defines it as a "Boy employed as a servant." There are two problems with these interpretations of the term "knave" in the context of this play, however. The first is that Shakespeare uses "knave" repeatedly throughout the play, and always in a context in which it is clear that it connotes a shameful identity and negative value judgment. In case there was any doubt, he uses "knave" interchangeably and in association with, or as essentially synonymous with, "villainy" and "treachery."

---

[1] Kermode (1974), p. 1255.   [2] Onions (1986), p. 149.

Gloucester's calling his bastard son Edmund a knave becomes, ironically and tragically, a self-fulfilling prophecy – though Gloucester is seemingly unaware of this at the opening of the play. For example, Edmund himself uses the term as one in a series of descriptions of people as "knaves, thieves and treachers" (i.e., treacherous persons), in which he includes also "villains," "fools," "drunkards, liars, and adulterers," and "all that we are evil in" (I.ii.122–6). But even if, as some critics suggest, Shakespeare intended the term to mean nothing more than that Edmund was a youthful male functioning as a servant, "knave" still implies that he occupied an inferior and shameful position. In his family he was seen as and would remain little more than a servant, whereas his half-brother Edgar would eventually become an Earl: a card-carrying member of the aristocracy. And as for being a "whoreson," Edmund and others use that term repeatedly in connection with women who are objects of shame, and Edmund refers to his father as a "whoremaster" – that is, a lecherous man who uses his superior power and position to pressure a woman into gratifying him sexually, thus treating her as a whore.

Thus at the very beginning of what many consider Shakespeare's greatest play, Gloucester refers to both his son Edmund and Edmund's mother in terms that reduce them to objects of shame, underscoring Edmund's inferiority to his half-brother Edgar. In this way Shakespeare introduces the perversion of parental love that impels the tragedy that follows.

It is true that Gloucester does say that Edgar, even though recognized "by order of law" as his son, is "no dearer in my account" than Edmund. Yet this assertion of love is belied and perverted by the fact that only Edgar, in his legitimacy, will inherit all the perquisites of being Gloucester's son. In this respect, Edgar clearly is "dearer" in Gloucester's "account" in terms of wealth, power, and status, as designated by the social and economic system of that time. For Edmund to believe that Edgar really was "no dearer" in his father's "account," he would virtually have to be out of touch with reality.

All of this is clarified by Edmund in the stunning soliloquy with which he opens the second scene of the play:

> Thou, Nature, art my goddess; to thy law
> My services are bound. Wherefore should I
> Stand in the plague of custom, and permit
> The curiosity [arbitrary laws] of nations to deprive me?
> For that I am some twelve or fourteen moonshines
> Lag of a brother? Why bastard? Wherefore base?
> When my dimensions are as well compact,

My mind as generous, and my shape as true
As honest [married, chaste] madam's issue? Why brand they us
With base? with baseness, bastardy? Base, base?...
Legitimate Edgar, I must have your land.
Our father's love is to the bastard Edmund
As to the legitimate. Fine word, "legitimate"!
Well, my legitimate, ... Edmund the base
Shall top the legitimate.

(I.ii.1–21)

Here he distinguishes between Nature, his "goddess," to whose natural laws (meaning his own intelligence and strengths) his "services are bound," and contrasts Nature, thus understood, with "the plague of custom," the human laws that will deprive him of what they will grant only to Edgar. He states that "Our father's love is to the bastard Edmund / As to the legitimate" Edgar. But these phrases are ambiguous enough to leave it unclear as to whether he means that his father's love is "owed" equally or "felt" equally with the love he gives to Edgar. In either case, he realizes that even his father has given human laws ("the plague of custom") priority over whatever his natural love of Edmund is. Hence Edgar is given priority of social status (wealth, lands, country house, and aristocratic rank – Edgar will inherit the title Earl of Gloucester). None of these accoutrements of status, wealth, and power will go to Edmund.

When we ask what motivates Edmund to murder and displace his father and his younger brother Edgar (his father's legal heir), the answer is clear: in contemporary terms, we call it a narcissistic injury. As he realizes, his bastardy constitutes, as the word itself implies, baseness and debasement, base or low status in a society that values what it calls "legitimacy." Edmund's soliloquy gives voice to his preoccupation with this reality, beginning as we have observed, with his allusion to the classical contrast between *physis* (nature, and the laws of nature) and *nomos* (human law, convention, custom).

If tragedy is the literary form in which guilt cultures critique the ethos of shame cultures, there could hardly be a clearer instance of this than in Edmund's soliloquy. For he is saying that despite the fact that even if his father has as much natural love for him as for his legitimate half-brother, he does not have enough love to remedy what he perceives as the social, legal, political, and economic injustice to himself as a consequence of his bastardy. Perceiving oneself as a victim of injustice, who is being unfairly relegated to an inferior status, is precisely what causes feelings of shame, and hence hate, and hence violence – which ultimately is inflicted on Edmund's father, Gloucester, with a degree of cruelty – pushing his eyes out of their sockets – that is horrifying even to contemplate, let alone witness on the stage. Or worse yet, recognize as something that real people did in reality, and still do.

But why attack the eyes? This does not happen just in plays, supposedly works of fiction. A twenty-year-old man in the United States was referred for a psychiatric evaluation after he had murdered a woman and stabbed out her eyes because, he said, "I didn't like the way she was looking at me." In interviews, he described (among other biographical details) how throughout his childhood he became the butt of bullies in school who taunted him with being "a wimp, a punk, and a pussy" (slang for a submissive coward, a passive homosexual, and a woman – all of which to him meant "not a man"), and felt looked down upon by his victim. Stabbing out her eyes was his way (following the rules of "magical thinking") of ending the shame caused by her (and everyone else) looking down on him, and observing his shame.

Another patient spent several years at a prison psychiatric hospital because he persisted in threatening, and attempting, to put out the eyes of other people. During his childhood, he had been forced to serve as a prostitute by a mother who served as his "pimp." Thus he was a "whore-son" in an even more literal way: a son who had been made into a (male) whore. His persisting wish to blind those around him followed logically – and psychologically – his wish to diminish the shame he felt over such an overwhelmingly degrading childhood.

For as Aristotle realized long ago, "shame dwells in the eyes." Shame is intensified when it is inflicted in front of others (as Edmund's was). Even when that is not the case, it is always perceived, and felt, as if it is being, or could be, observed by an audience. To feel shamed is to feel looked down upon by others; thus, people feel shamed in the eyes of others, who can see your shame. The poet Carl Sandburg used to sing an old American folk song about a murderer standing under the gallows waiting to be hanged who sings, "My name it is Sam Hall, And I hate you one and all, *God damn your eyes.*"

Shakespeare's depiction of Edmund's behavior in *King Lear* is a psycho-logically perceptive and accurate dramatization of how and why people attempt to protect themselves from being shamed, by means of magical thinking: as if by putting out the eyes of the person who is shaming you, you can end the shaming. From that standpoint, this grotesque form of violence is neither arbitrary nor incomprehensible.

As for Lear, speaking of his daughter Cordelia before banishing her from his kingdom, he says, "*I lov'd her most*, and thought to set my rest on her kind nursery" (I.i.123–4). The most important word in this sentence is "most," conveying Lear's open acknowledgment that he loved Cordelia more than he loved her sisters, Goneril and Regan. Both of them were present to hear this confirmation of a conclusion, devastating to them, that they had already intuited. In addition, the term "set my rest" means to "stake my all," a term from the card game Primero, which could imply that he was prepared to give Cordelia his whole estate and all his love, until she refused to say that she would love him more than she would her husband; though it might also be interpreted merely to mean that he intended to depend for his repose – his retirement – on her loving care. But even that implies that he wanted to reverse the parent–child relationship, asking her not to act like his daughter but to act as if she were his mother and he was the child – for nursing, and nurseries, are, after all, the domain of the mother with an infant. So Lear was abdicating his responsibility as the parent in two ways: in expecting Cordelia to care for him as if she were the parent and then, in rejecting her, refusing to act as her parent. But by that point he had already clearly communicated to his other daughters that he loved Cordelia more than he loved them.

One of the ironies in this speech is that when he goes on to say, "So be my grave my peace," he is foretelling what would happen later far more accurately than he recognized at the time – for he would in fact find peace only when he finally descended to his grave. For what was actually most destructive to Lear was not only that he disowned Cordelia; he also openly shamed Goneril and Regan. As Goneril says to Regan, "He always lov'd our sister most" (I.i.290). And even Cordelia's husband-to-be, the King of France, recognizes and acknowledges this, when he describes Cordelia as "she, whom even but now was your [best] object, / The argument of your praise, balm of your age, / The best, the dearest" (I.i.214–16). The fact that Shakespeare states this same thought three times, in the mouths of three different characters, and right at the beginning of the play, suggests that he wants to make sure that we do not miss the point.

Lear also foments the rivalry between his daughters when he asks Cordelia, "What can you say to draw a third [of his kingdom] more opulent than your sisters?" (I.i.85–6). And by stirring up the rivalry, he provokes resentment toward him on the part of his two less loved daughters, which ultimately turns them against both him and Cordelia.

But if we ask why Lear rejects Cordelia, apart from the obvious reason that she refuses to profess her love for him with the same effusiveness as her sisters, Lear himself leads us to the answer when he refers to her as "a wretch whom Nature" (meaning *his* nature) "is asham'd / Almost t'acknowledge hers." He himself had felt shamed by her unwillingness to say that she loved him more than any other person on earth. But only someone who lacks sufficient love for himself would need such an affirmation of unreasonable, unlimited love from another person.

Nevertheless, Lear does show a remarkable capacity for growth in that his ultimate response to his suffering is to recognize the utter failure and destructiveness, including self-destructiveness, of his original strategy for living, including his plan for how and why to divide up his kingdom (by criteria based on his own egocentricity, not generosity). He finally achieves the capacity to identify with the underdog, the homeless and hungry, poor and unclothed, rather than with the ruling class, which is precisely what he had been the ruler of, up to then:

> Poor naked wretches, wheresoe'er you are,
> That bide the pelting of this pitiless storm,
> How shall your houseless heads and unfed sides,
> Your loop'd and window'd raggedness, defend you
> From seasons such as this! Take physic, pomp;
> Expose thyself to what wretches feel,
> That thou mayst shake the superflux to them,
> And show the heavens more just.
>
> (III.iv.28–36)

By the end of the play, Lear has reversed his whole conception of justice from that of a shame ethic to that of a guilt ethic. In response to the realization that all of his original assumptions about human relationships have proven false or mistaken, and with the help of the fool and of Edgar, disguised as poor Tom, who stay with him in his madness, Lear outgrows the shame ethic with its attempt to compensate for the lack of self-love that shame consists of, and develops the capacity to love others. That finally enables him to recognize the ultimate equality of all human beings, from kings to beggars and madmen, in their capacity for suffering, their vulnerability to humiliation, and their need for compassion, and to register his own culpability, in having failed to do more to relieve the suffering of others.

Part of what makes this play a tragedy is that by that point it is too late to undo the emotional and physical damage that Lear has already caused, both to himself and to all the other major characters in the play. Yes, he has achieved the salvation of his own soul, his own self. But his previous follies, his colossal misunderstanding of both himself and everyone else, have consequences that even his internal transformation cannot undo or prevent. In what Greek tragedy would call necessity (*Ananke*), and what the modern scientific age calls the necessity with which causes produce effects, Lear is not exempted from the consequences of his own previous, truly tragic, mistakes and errors: for even Cordelia dies, which makes his own death, ultimately, the only means by which his suffering could come to an end.

The tragedy of *King Lear* thus dramatizes the case of two fathers who stumble or bumble into shaming their children, blind to (and blinded by) the consequences that will follow, and who then, after suffering those consequences – Lear's banishment and Gloucester's blinding – are finally able to see the costs of the shame ethic that previously had driven their actions as parents. Lear may well be the greatest of Shakespeare's tragedies in that it is arguably the most devastating critique guilt ethics and guilt cultures can make of shame ethics and shame cultures: the perversion of love that leads a parent to shame his children (in the name of justice and law), with results that are lethal to both parent and child. The play depicts unnatural acts, a perversion of normal and healthy parental love, driven by the customs or laws of a country where questions of legitimacy take precedence over loving feelings, and where flattery (to satisfy a father's vanity) is mistaken for love.

In *Coriolanus*, it is a mother in whom we see the perversion of love. Shakespeare puts Volumnia under his microscope, a mother who goes to great lengths to teach her son that the way for him to avoid shame and achieve pride and honor instead is by killing as many of the enemies of the city as possible. He is to become a killing machine, and his honor will also be her honor, the pride she will feel as the mother of such a heroic son. She is willing to accept that he will thus expose himself to the certainty of being wounded and the risk of being killed.

Talking with Virgilia, Coriolanus's wife, Volumnia recounts in great detail how she raised Coriolanus and why. He is currently away at war, and Volumnia explains why Virgilia should neither complain nor worry about his absence, and why she should value honor over love:

> If my son were my husband, I should freelier rejoice in that absence wherein he won honor than in the embracements of his bed where he would show most love. When yet he was but tender-bodied and the only son of my womb, when youth with comeliness pluck'd all gaze his way, when for a day of kings' entreaties a mother should not sell him an hour from her beholding, I, considering how honor would become such a person, . . . was pleas'd to let him seek danger where he was like to find fame. To a cruel war I sent him, from whence he return'd, with brows bound with oak. I tell thee, daughter, I sprang not more in joy at first hearing he was a man-child than now seeing he had prov'd himself a man.

To which Virgilia responds, "But had he died in the business, madam, how then?" Volumnia is undeterred:

> Then his good report should have been my son; I therein would have found issue. Hear me profess sincerely: had I a dozen sons, each in my love alike, and none less dear than thine and my good Martius, I had rather had eleven die nobly for their country than one voluptuously surfeit out of action. (I.iii.2–25)

Soon after, Volumnia says to Virgilia:

> Methinks I hear your husband's drum,
> See him pluck Aufidius [the leader of the Volscians] down by th' hair;
>   As children from a bear, the Volsces shunning him,
> Methinks I see him stamp thus, and call thus [to his own troops]
>   "Come on, you cowards, you were got in fear,
> Though you were born in Rome!" His bloody brow
> With his mail'd hand then wiping, forth he goes,
> Like to a harvest-man task'd to mow
> Or all or lose his hire.

To which Virgilia then exclaims, "His bloody brow? O Jupiter, no blood!" Volumnia's response leaves no question with regard to the ethos in which she had raised her son, where the spilling of blood is a badge of honor:

> Away, you fool! It more becomes a man
> Than gilt his trophy. The breasts of Hecuba
> When she did suckle Hector, look'd not lovelier
> Than Hector's forehead when it spit forth blood
> At Grecian sword.
>
>   (I.iii.29–43)

How are we to understand this? While we can hardly miss the Oedipal/incestuous overtones of her reference to how she would feel if her son were her husband, we do not consider this the most significant aspect of her depiction of how she brought him up. More relevant in the sense of explaining his overweening commitment to violence, and the pride and honor it brings with it, is the fact that she places greater value on his honor and fame than on his life – and teaches him to do the same.

We find two other important implications in the first of her speeches quoted above. The first is that she shares the assumption common to shame cultures, that within the patriarchal construction of masculinity, a male child will not become a man just by growing up. Manhood requires him to prove that he is a man – a "real" man – by displaying courage and achieving pride and honor, which in the terms of the play he can do only by means of violence against others. Within patriarchy, a man's adequacy as a member of the male sex is always fragile, contestable, and contingent on the degree to which he is able and willing to be violent, under many well-defined circumstances.

It is no accident, then, that the words for "masculinity," in both Greek and Latin, also mean "courage": in Greek, *andreia* (the root of our word "androgen"); and in Latin, *virtus*, the root of our word "virtue" – though in Latin it means courage. For in the warlike culture of ancient Greece and Rome (even classical Athens, despite creating a nascent guilt culture, retained enough features of its traditional shame culture to remain both militaristic and imperialistic), the chief virtue, the chief requirement for being a man, that is, a warrior, was courage. For you could not attempt to kill the enemy without subjecting yourself to the fact that they will be just as determined to kill you. So a prerequisite for manhood, at least for manly, honorable violence against one's equals and peers, is courage. And in Rome the root of *virtus* was *vir*, which means both "man" and "soldier" – which again is hardly surprising, since all soldiers had to be men, not women, and most able-bodied men could well be expected and even required to serve as soldiers. The words "virile" and "virility" are of course also derivatives of *vir*, and are thus associated with masculinity, courage, militarism, and aggressiveness.

The second implication that Volumnia articulates is the assumption, again common to shame cultures, that women cannot be the source of honor; only men can. In such cultures, a woman can gain honor only by having an intimate relationship with a man of honor – whereas a man can gain honor only by his own achievements and behavior (and that of his family), not by entering into a relationship with a "woman of honor." In fact, that latter term is something of a misnomer, for honor in cultures of shame and honor is not conceived as actually belonging to a woman intrinsically, in herself as a separate individual. It is important in such cultures to have a woman's "honor" respected, but that is only because her honor is actually understood as belonging not to herself but to the men in her family: her father, brothers, husband, or sons. If a woman is dishonored, disrespected, or shamed, either by her own behavior (e.g., sexual behavior with anyone other than her husband) or by another person (e.g., rape), that dishonors the men in her family, which can be restored only by means of an "honor killing."

Thus Volumnia can gain honor only as it is reflected from her son onto her, which is a major reason such a mother would want her son to do what he does. It serves her narcissistic gratification, her pride, as much as his.

And to achieve this, she is perfectly happy to have her son subjected to injuries, including lethal ones. That is why we call this a perversion of maternal love.

This psychological and cultural phenomenon is by no means limited to *Coriolanus*. Two inmates, brothers, who were imprisoned in Massachusetts for a series of bank robberies recounted that their mother was ashamed of them for letting themselves be taken alive. In her eyes, they would have been real men only if they had died in a shootout with the police, in the manner of Bonnie and Clyde, John Dillinger, et al. Instead, here they were in the shameful position of being imprisoned, failures as bank robbers, as men, and hence as sons.

In his book *Southern Honor*, the historian Bertram Wyatt-Brown writes about the American South as a shame culture. In doing so, he underscores the role of mothers in initiating their sons into its culture of violence and the preference for death over dishonor. During the War of 1812, for example, Sam Houston joined the army. His mother, who had urged him to do so, handed him a musket, saying, "Never disgrace it; for remember, I had rather all my sons should fill one honorable grave, than that one of them should turn his back to save his life." Then she presented him with a plain gold ring, with the word "honor" engraved inside it.[3]

The ultimate tragedy of *Coriolanus* for both mother and son is that she has raised him to be so hypersensitive to any slights to his pride that he insults the common people of Rome by insisting on his superiority to them. By thus dishonoring them, he provokes them into dishonoring him, which they do by refusing to grant him his consulship and banishing him from the city. This then results in a cascading series of catastrophes that lead finally to his death.

In *Henry VI*, we saw how a guilt-sensitive monarch is destroyed by the shame culture in which he lives. With *Coriolanus*, we see the reverse: how a shame-driven personality cannot survive in a culture that has moved at least partway toward democracy (rule by the common people). Shakespeare thus alerts us not to underestimate what is at stake when these two moral value systems and cultural patterns collide against one another. In both plays, it is a matter of life or death – as it is in real life.

What Shakespeare also shows us in *King Lear* and *Coriolanus* are the perversions of parental love that are virtually universal in shame cultures and contribute to their violence. It would be hard to find a more detailed, exact, and psychologically astute depiction of the forces that lead parents to

---

[3] Wyatt-Brown (1982), p. 51.

shame their children or teach them to prefer death to dishonor. As we see in these plays, the result is catastrophic for both parent and child.

In the final quatrain of *King Lear*, when Albany says, "The wisdom of this sad time we must obey, Speak what we feel, not what we ought to say," our sense of having witnessed something unnatural returns. With these lines, Shakespeare calls our attention to how cultural mores can override human nature, so that rather than speaking what they feel, people say what they have been taught they ought to say. Hence, the perversion of love.

CHAPTER 4

Make War, Not Love
Antony and Cleopatra

Whereas Falstaff may be seen as a character who never developed a capacity for feeling either shame or guilt, Antony and Cleopatra transcend both, ascending into "a new heaven and a new earth" of love on a scale the magnitude of which is truly magnificent. The play leaves both shame and guilt far below them, diminished into irrelevance. Tragedy is the story of how shame engenders guilt by motivating violence, which ultimately destroys both the tragic hero and his victim(s). Although Antony initially does feel shame (over having foolishly lost the battle of Actium), that is far from becoming his central tragedy. That mistake ultimately loses its centrality in his estimation of himself and his life, because it is so far outweighed by his love for Cleopatra – compared with which nothing can be considered of comparable importance or relevance, even the difference between life and death. The two lovers, for whom the rest of life disappeared whenever they were together, ultimately stay together when life itself disappears; in fact, they realize they can stay together only by dying together.

To them, the difference between life and death cannot even be compared with the immeasurably greater difference between remaining together versus separating from each other. For each, life without the other would not be life, and death simply happens to be the only means by which they can remain united. So they accept it without regret, as bringing a greater reward than mere physical survival alone could possibly do, thus constituting a greater victory in itself.

This is the sense in which Antony and Cleopatra can be said to transcend tragedy, which is always about the conflict between shame and guilt, love and hate, life and death. They are, to each other, all there is of life, and so they join with each other in death. They transcend their military defeat in the ultimate victory of their love for each other. Thus for them there is no conflict between life versus death, shame versus guilt, love versus hate, or victory versus defeat.

There are characters and institutions in this play that do represent shame and guilt, and the difference between them. Octavius Caesar is the perfectly successful shame-driven apparatchik – the autocrat as bureaucrat, whose all-consuming will to power represents all the emotional depth of which he is capable. Yet because of that he succeeds in attaining the pride of empire by killing or otherwise defeating all his rivals in order to ascend to his throne as the first Emperor of Rome, and whose very title, Augustus, will celebrate the august heights to which he has risen. But he remains an infinitely smaller person than the two lovers whom he thought he had defeated – only to discover that they had defeated him instead, precisely by dying – as he himself realizes and admits. He has not triumphed over them – they have prevented that by the very act of dying, by which they have triumphed over him. He remains alive, of course; but the life he lives, for all its martial and material glory, is more cramped and limited than the magnitude of the passion with which Antony and Cleopatra both live and die with each other, on a scale and intensity of aliveness that Octavius gives no indication of ever having the capacity for. In fact, he gives no hint of possessing anything more profound than the personality that was needed, created by, and rewarded by the shame culture and the shame-driven politics of the world in which he lived: the Roman Empire, created and sustained by Roman soldiers.

That was also the world in which Antony grew up and whose values he absorbed and acted on, to great success – until he discovered something more valuable by whole orders of magnitude, which was incompatible with, and could ultimately not survive in, the militaristic, imperialistic, authoritarian, genocidal shame culture that produced and maintained the Roman Empire (until that Empire finally imploded and collapsed from the very vacuity, superficiality, and self-destructiveness of its values). What is truly tragic in this play – the real tragedy it shows us – is the tragedy that is imposed on whole nations, by the incompatibility between the emotionally shallow and morally primitive shame culture that Shakespeare shows us here, and the capacity for love that Antony and Cleopatra exhibit.

Again, we are not saying that Shakespeare was preaching to us, or spinning an abstract theoretical argument, about the incompatibility between the political system depicted in this play (which was not different, in any relevant way, from that of Shakespeare's England, or the many dictatorships of our own world) and the intensity of love that the lovers in this play are revealing as among the potentialities inherent in human nature, if we do not strangle it. As Harold Bloom observes, "Shakespeare, as always, does not let us see whether he himself prefers one side or the other, but the contrast among the perpetual intensity of Cleopatra, the dying music of Antony, and the grumpy efficiency of Octavius Caesar can lead us to a probable surmise on the poet's preferences."[1]

So, yes, the play does show us a tragedy – but the true victims of the "make war, not love" culture of Rome and Augustus are much more those ostensible victors and their compatriots and descendants than are the two lovers for whom the play is named.

We realize that the plot of this play conforms to the pattern of what has been called "romantic love," as described by numerous authors from Stendhal[2] to Denis de Rougemont.[3] As they describe it, this form of love can exist only outside marriage, either premarital (for which Romeo and Juliet could serve as an example) or extra-marital, that is, adulterous (as in Tristan and Isolde, Anna Karenina, and this play, among hundreds of others). And it always ends in, and indeed requires, the death of one or both lovers – hence the "love-death" of *Tristan*, the suicide of the lovers in this play, and others.

But while these are all exemplified in *Antony and Cleopatra*, we feel that to reduce the play to this formula underestimates the play's power and significance. Shakespeare is delivering a critique of the whole social world that makes Antony and Cleopatra's love impossible, and in this sense makes much of the human capacity for love – and life – impossible. Yes, Stendhal, de Rougemont, and others give a plausible explanation for why romantic love came into existence and was incompatible with marriage, both in the ancient world and in the medieval world which Europe was just beginning to outgrow during the time Shakespeare was writing: namely, the fact that marriages in the world of monarchies and aristocracies were primarily arranged marriages – and arranged not to facilitate a love relationship between the two spouses. Rather, the intention was to effect a dynastic political, economic, and military union between two families or nations, in order to turn them from rivals into allies (as Antony experienced in both of his marriages, to Fulvia and Octavia). And under these circumstances, the only sphere in which personal love was likely to arise spontaneously was outside marriage. This then appears to be one more reason for ending the social and political systems called monarchy and aristocracy.

Yet we have also seen, in our own era, how marriages can also be "adulterated" by financial, ethnic, religious, and other forces outside the

---

relation of the couple themselves that may have the same effect, namely, of distracting or inhibiting people from the full capacity for love of which humans are capable. This, again, is simply another argument in favor of reducing those impediments and distractions to the greatest degree possible, especially when we realize that love is the antithesis of both shame and guilt and therefore the key to overcoming violence.

Of all the characters in this play, Enobarbus is the only example of a person consumed by feelings of guilt. After he has abandoned and betrayed Antony, but then, despite that, been rewarded by Antony with generous and uncalled-for material gifts, he comments that "I am alone the villain of the earth, And feel I am so most" (i.e., I am myself the person most painfully aware of the fact). "O Antony, . . . how wouldst thou have paid My better service, when my turpitude Thou dost so crown with gold! This blows my heart" (or "swells my heart to point of bursting"). "I Fight against thee? No, I will go seek / Some ditch wherein to die; the foul'st best fits My latter part of life" (IV.ix.7–10). He then goes on to say, "Be witness to me, O thou blessed moon, . . . poor Enobarbus did Before thy face repent."

It is important not to confuse his suicide with that of Antony and Cleopatra. Enobarbus' suicide is motivated by guilt feelings, theirs by the refusal to submit themselves to the shame of being exhibited to the people of Rome as objects of shame in Caesar's "triumph." Yet we cannot help but feel that their love for each other was the predominant motive for their mutual suicides. Yes, Antony cites what he has been told (falsely) of Cleopatra's suicide as making him feel shamed and dishonorable not to have shown the same courage she has shown in killing herself. But he would not have cared so much about her behavior in the first place if he had not loved and admired her so much. So his shame was the product of feeling he had not lived up to the standards of his beloved, not that he needed to kill himself merely to avoid being shamed by Caesar.

The clearest contrast to Antony's behavior, in fact, is another poem describing the origins of the Roman Empire, the *Aeneid*. In that epic poem, Virgil describes how Aeneas decides that he must make war, not love, even though that constitutes a shame-inducing betrayal of Dido, the woman he has loved and who has loved him. This is so painful for her that she kills herself. She does so not in order to remain close to Aeneas, but because she realizes that no matter what she does, she has been rejected by him in favor of his shame-motivated violent ambitions.

The exact opposite is true of Antony's behavior and character. Antony loses the battle with Caesar because he has chosen to make love, not war. That this choice constitutes his priority – "Let Rome in Tiber melt and the wide arch / Of the ranged Empire fall. Here is my space" **"Kingdoms are clay; our dungy earth alike Feeds beast as man; the nobleness of life Is to do thus [*embracing Cleopatra*] – when such a mutual pair And such a twain can don't, ... We stand up peerless." (I.i.33–40)** – is the clearest indication of how completely Antony rejects the value system of the shame ethic of both his and Shakespeare's time (and of how little room there is in such a culture for love between two persons).

CHAPTER 5

The Motives of Malignity
Shame and Masculinity in Othello and Macbeth

Among the most interesting findings from the circum-Mediterranean culture area (which includes Venice and also North Africa, from which Othello came), as well as from the former slave-owning states of the "Old South" in the United States, is that men and women stand in a markedly different relationship to the whole system of allotting honor in these "shame and honor cultures." For example, men are the only sources, or active generators, of honor. The only effect women can have on honor in these cultures is to destroy it. But women do have that power: they can destroy their own honor, and when they do that they also destroy the honor of the men in their household. The way they do this is by engaging in sex outside marriage. That is, by being "unchaste."

The French sociologist Pierre Bourdieu, writing about North African culture, observes that "Everything occurs as if the woman could not really increase the honour of the agnates" (the male members of her extended patriarchal family), "but only preserve it intact by her good conduct and respectability, or destroy it (*ekes elaardh*, take away one's reputation) by her misconduct."[1]

As we cannot understand violence without understanding shame, it is also true that we cannot understand shame without grasping the definition of masculine and feminine identities that underlies the honor/shame syndrome in culture. To put it simply, shaming a man puts his manhood at risk – that is, his manhood as defined by that culture.

Shakespeare knew this. In *Othello* and *Macbeth*, he dramatizes the ways in which a man can be shamed and thus incited by others to commit murders they would never have done on their own. In both tragedies, shame deforms the character of the tragic hero; in Aristotle's terms, his sensitivity to shame is his tragic flaw. Othello is tricked by Iago into believing that Desdemona, his wife, has been unfaithful to him.

[1] In Gilmore (1987), p. 241.

Macbeth is goaded by his wife into believing he will not really be a man unless he murders Duncan, the king. In both instances, the motivation is the desire to undo or avoid shame – in Othello's case, the shame of being a cuckold; in Macbeth's case, the shame of being a coward. The murder, whether of Desdemona or of Duncan, signifies an attempt to restore manhood and thereby regain honor.

As the anthropologist Julian Pitt-Rivers put it,[2] "The ultimate vindication of honour lies in physical violence and when other means fail, the obligation exists, not only in the formal code of honour but in social milieux which admit no such code, to revert to it.... By showing his readiness to fight, a man restored his honour . . . honour was particularly to be earned through military prowess."

The cultural historian Bertram Wyatt-Brown, writing about the American South as a "culture of honor," was similarly struck by "the centrality of violence as opposed to other forms of criminal behavior, for the maintenance of personal honor."[3] But this was also the motive for violence to maintain national honor: "It was threat of honor lost, no less than slavery, that led [the Southern states] to secession and war."[4]

And Pierre Bourdieu, describing Kabyle society (in the Maghreb/North Africa – the area from which Othello came), which is marked by endemic intertribal warfare, feuds and vendettas, professional assassins and blood vengeance, pointed out that

> The person who fails to take revenge ceases to exist for other people. This is why the most worthless man has always enough *h'achma* [sensitivity to shame], to avenge himself. The formulas employed when speaking of dishonour are significant: "How shall I be able to appear before people?" . . . "My life is over!" A man's honour is his own honour. In him, existence and honour are one. He who has lost his honour no longer exists. He ceases to exist for other people, and at the same time he ceases to exist for himself.[5]

These are perfect descriptions of Othello. In addition, contrary to Coleridge's description of Iago as exemplifying "motiveless malignity," Shakespeare makes it clear that Iago is motivated to destroy Othello by the shame and hence hate that he felt over Othello's having passed him over for promotion and giving the captainship instead to Cassio (who had less seniority and less experience in battle). Iago also believed that Othello had seduced Emilia, Iago's wife. By naming Cassio as the one who had

---

[2] Pitt-Rivers (1966), p. 29. See also Pitt-Rivers (1968).   [3] Wyatt-Brown (1982), p. 366.
[4] Ibid., p. 5.   [5] In Gilmore (1987).

given Othello his "horns," Iago was seeking to undo both of his own humiliations by means of one integrated strategy of revenge that would destroy both of the men by whom he felt humiliated.

Whether or not Iago's suspicion was true – that Othello had cuckolded him by having an affair with his wife – it is still the case that both he and Othello illustrate very clearly how men in the shame culture in which this tragedy unfolds are hypersensitive to slights to their pride and honor, which elicit feelings of being shamed and dishonored, which stimulate feelings of hate, along with the belief that the only way to undo the shame and dishonor is by committing an "honor killing" of the offending party or parties.

The effect that Iago's shaming of Othello has is consistent with the effect that Iago's own feelings of shame have had on him. On the principle that "it takes one to know one," Iago shows exquisitely sensitive and subtle intuitions as to how to make even the most noncredible accusations against Desdemona credible to Othello, and thereby shame-inducing, and therefore violence-inducing: a sequence of events that are among the saddest and most painful to witness in all of Shakespeare's plays, given how effectively they destroy two otherwise blameless and admirable people – Othello and Desdemona.

The most significant difference between Othello and Iago is that Othello does have the capacity to feel love toward someone other than himself, which means he also has the capacity to feel guilty over harming that person. Even with Othello, however, there are serious gaps in the integrity of his conscience. The first is that he felt guilty for killing Desdemona only when he discovered that in fact she had been faithful to him. This leaves open the implication that had she actually been having an affair with Cassio, she would have been guilty of dishonoring Othello and he would have been justified in murdering her as an "honor-killing." Thus it is left ambiguous as to how partially or completely Othello had truly transcended and freed himself from the shame ethic of the culture in which he lived (to the degree that Marc Antony had, for example).

The other self-exculpation Othello indulges in lies in describing himself as "An honourable murderer, if you will: For naught I did in hate, but all in honour" (V.ii. 2934–5). In this speech, Othello appears to be aware that people might blame or criticize him had he been motivated by hate rather than by honor. In fact, he was motivated both by hate and by honor – for he thought Desdemona had dishonored him by cuckolding him, and it was that belief, joined with his love of honor and hatred of dishonor, that caused him to hate her.

But this is also a play about ambivalence: for he felt both hate and love toward both Desdemona and himself. He killed her because he hated her, and hated her because he loved her (which was what made her putative infidelity, i.e., her transfer of her love from him to Cassio, so intolerably shameful, and therefore painful, to him), and killed her in order to regain his self-love, or honor; and hated himself for having killed her, because he still loved her, so he killed himself as well. Nevertheless, in the end, even though professing his love for Desdemona, it is clear that honor and manhood remained his overriding concerns, outweighing even his love for her. This despite his earlier claim, "if honour outlive honesty, let it go all."

One might ask whether in acknowledging that he had murdered Desdemona for the sake of honor, Othello is deceiving himself and those to whom he is speaking by denying that he killed her because of his hatred of her. And by this denial, is he claiming that despite having killed her, he still loved her, as he implies when he tells the Venetians, "Then you must speak of me as one who loved not wisely but too well" (meaning, we think, "too intensely" – i.e., so intensely that it made him vulnerable to more pain than he was able to bear, when he believed she no longer loved him)?

To answer these questions, it is necessary to recognize that in loving Desdemona and then believing himself to have lost the love she had felt for him when she supposedly became involved with Cassio, Othello had become vulnerable to some of the most painful feelings that people can experience: sadness and shame, including the variety of shame called jealousy. His response to experiencing these feelings becomes apparent when he tells us, "I am abuse'd, and my relief / Must be to loathe her" (III.iii.270–1). Here Othello reveals that it is a relief to replace loving with loathing, thereby conveying that loathing (hating) is a defense against the pain of loving. To take this a step further, the fact that you are defending yourself against a feeling (in this case, love) that brings you pain does not mean that you don't have that feeling; instead, it means that you are trying to relieve the pain of having the feeling. Replacing love with hate is completely different from simply not loving or being indifferent, for hating in this context is a means of repressing the source of pain, one's love, and thus deceiving oneself, or pretending to oneself, that one does not have the feeling that one actually (unconsciously) has. Prior to killing Desdemona, Othello several times states how much he hates her; indeed, that is the only way he can rationalize to himself what his motive is for killing her.

As Freud pointed out, the repressed or defended-against feeling or thought does still exist, and not only exists, but will return, albeit usually in a disguised form. To Freud, the return of the repressed is what constitutes the form that psychopathology takes. In Othello's case, his repressed love for Desdemona returns in the disguised (and pathological, meaning life-destroying) form of hate and murder. For hate is simply love turned inside out, so to speak; it actually mimics love in every detail, though in reverse. Hate, like love, is the opposite of indifference, in that both lovers and haters are obsessed with the object of their feeling, and almost cannot think of anyone else. Nor can they leave the object of their emotion alone; they feel compelled to interact with that person, whether to bring pleasure or pain, to enhance the person's life or to end it.

Seen in this light, Othello is both telling the truth and telling an untruth when he says that he loved Desdemona and when he said that he hated her. For he had both feelings, and they both were conscious at some points and unconscious at others. Loving and hating the same person at the same time – and not only at the same time, but for the same reasons – is the very definition of ambivalence. To Othello, Desdemona was irresistibly lovable, attractive both physically and in her character; in other words, he loved her for being the person she was. But, with an irony that reached tragic dimensions, this is precisely what made Othello hate her: because he loved her, and this in turn made him more vulnerable to emotional pain than any other feeling can. He hated her because he loved her and he hated her because in inducing him to love her, she had induced him to allow himself to become vulnerable to being hurt by her.

But Othello would not have been as vulnerable as he was had he not lived in a shame culture that made it more shameful for him to love than to hate and to kill. And furthermore, it was a culture that could inflict shame of such intensity on men that it could provoke, as in the case of Othello, what was tantamount to the death of the self. Within a shame culture, then, the following equations prevail (for men): violence = courage = honor = masculinity = the viability, even existence, of one's self. And masculinity (in a shame culture) = male dominance = patriarchy, without which men in shame cultures feel they are not men – hence their self (defined as being a man) no longer exists.

The dynamic relationship between shame, guilt, and violence (shame leading to anger at others and punishment of them, and guilt to self-punishment) is laid out clearly by Shakespeare in the tragedy of *Othello*. After Iago has exposed Othello to shame by deceiving him into believing that Desdemona had dishonored him by making him into an object of scorn and ridicule – a cuckold – Othello murders Desdemona. He then commits suicide, after praying to be punished in hell ("Whip me, ye devils, ... roast me in sulphur! Wash me in steep-down gulfs of liquid fire!"), having discovered that he had been guilty of killing an innocent person who had actually loved him (and whom he had loved).

But the tragic flaw of guilt ethics, as Shakespeare dramatizes in this play, is that it does not solve the problem that violence poses for human survival. Although guilt ethics replaces hate and violence toward others with commandments to love and care for them, it also replaces hate and violence toward others with commandments to direct hate and violence toward the self when one feels guilty – as Othello does, who stabs himself to death.

We might well wonder why Othello was so vulnerable to being persuaded by Iago to doubt the innocent Desdemona's fidelity to him and to abandon his own powerful love for her. Othello himself mentions, among the reasons why she might have preferred another man to him, his race, his greater age, and his lack of the kinds of verbal and social skills that he assumed were available to some of the younger gallants who were also part of her social world. But he dismissed these as not likely to lead her to abandon her love for him, and the Doge (Duke) of Venice himself stated why it was completely credible that Desdemona herself would have fallen in love with Othello, and that their racial difference was irrelevant.

It is difficult to find any major reasons in the text of the play for how credulous Othello was about even the most fantastic false accusations Iago made against Desdemona, apart from the construction of sexual relations that are characteristic of shame cultures. These include the assumption of male supremacy, which can also be referred to as male domination or male chauvinism, sexism, or misogyny, and is the sine qua non of patriarchy, an order of living structured around the privileging of fathers. This is one version of the assumption that the human world is divided into the superior (the proud and honorable) and the inferior (the shameful and dishonored). The hierarchical, patriarchal construction of society includes the assumption that men are superior and women inferior and that to be a real man, meaning a man of honor, one has to be superior to other men as well – stronger, more dominant, and, when others refuse to be subservient, more violent. As a result, this patriarchal code of honor, which is a central component in the ethos of a shame culture, becomes a recipe for violence generally.

Any man who allows a woman in his family or personal relationships – a wife, daughter, sister, lover, even mother (as with Hamlet) – to refuse to do whatever he tells her to do (especially to obey the Seventh Commandment, "Thou shalt not commit adultery") is, as a result, socially and psychologically emasculated, with his reputation and hence his sense of self in the eyes of others tarnished if not destroyed. For he is a man, and if his manhood is destroyed, he is destroyed. In shame cultures, men are defined as superior to women, and for a man to fail to enforce this hierarchy is to lose his manhood, meaning his identity, his personhood.

Macbeth

As we have said, tragedy can be seen as a critique of shame ethics by guilt ethics. More specifically, Shakespeare's tragedies dramatize the cost of shame ethics to the men for whom the plays are named: Hamlet, Othello, King Lear, and perhaps above all, Macbeth, a noble thane and loyal subject of his king. Nowhere is Shakespeare's poetry more compressed – "Come seeling night, scarf up the tender eye of pitiful day" – or more precise in forecasting the tragedy to come: the overcoming of guilt by shame.

It is also true that nowhere in Shakespeare's canon are the gender dynamics of a patriarchal order more clearly exposed. In the very first message – the letter – that Macbeth sends to his wife, he tells her that witches have prophesied that he would become king. "Dearest partner of greatness," he writes, informing her "of what greatness is promis'd thee." By his becoming king, she would become the queen; the increase in his honor and stature would increase hers as well. In fact, it is her only access to such recognition, and thus the stage is set for what follows: her determination to ensure that he will become "what thou art promis'd."

However, there is one impediment, which she clearly states: "I fear thy nature. It is too full o' the milk of human kindness / To catch the nearest way" (I.v.17–19). Here she not only sets out the conflict between nature and murder, or more precisely, between Macbeth's nature and his and her ambition that he become King, but she implicitly divides nature into the masculine and the feminine, saying in effect that her husband's masculine aspiration (and hers for him) to become the king is at odds with his feminine nature, his kindness (as if kindness is incompatible with masculinity), for it is only women and more specifically mothers who can produce milk. Thus Lady Macbeth throws down the gauntlet: Macbeth's manhood is at stake.

In highlighting the costs and the consequences of patriarchy for men as well as for women, I (David Richards) have underscored how the gender binary divides men from those aspects of their human nature that are gendered "feminine," and the patriarchal gender hierarchy, the privileging of the so-called masculine qualities, shames men for possessing any characteristics that are defined as "feminine."[6] The gender binary and hierarchy are in fact the building blocks, "the DNA of a patriarchal order,"[7] and no one has observed this with greater precision than Shakespeare's character Lady Macbeth. As she tells her husband, "Thou wouldst be great; /Art not without ambition, but without / The illness [wickedness] should attend it."

Since Shakespeare's time, psychoanalysts including Ernest Jones and Otto Fenichel have noted that ambition is specifically stimulated by shame. To recall Fenichel's observation, "the aim of ambition ... is to prove that there is no need to be ashamed anymore."[8] He also noticed that "the 'success' which is the goal of ambition may acquire the meaning of killing ... and therefore," in those who are capable of guilt feelings, "become prohibited."[9] Lady Macbeth anticipated these discoveries by centuries. As we have seen, she has noticed Macbeth's refusal to honor the demands that shame ethics makes on men to behave in ways that guilt ethics forbids. She has called this refusal on his part his absence of an "illness" (what today we might call psychopathy or sociopathy, although in Shakespeare's time the word may have connoted "evil" or "wickedness"). Continuing on the same theme, she tells him, "What thou wouldst [achieve] highly / That wouldst thou [do] holily"; that is, he "wouldst not play false."

Thus Lady Macbeth resolves to "pour my spirits in thine ear, / And chastise with the valor of my tongue, / All that impedes thee" – namely, Macbeth's guilt feelings, including the obligation he feels to be honest, loyal, and nonviolent toward his king (I.iv.16–30). And chastise she does! As persistently as Iago did with Othello and just as skillfully and success-fully, Lady Macbeth incites Macbeth to overcome his guilt-motivated inhibitions against committing murder by mercilessly shaming him – by questioning his masculinity whenever he hesitates to commit whatever violence is needed in order to realize his (and her) ambitions.

"Wouldst thou have that / Which thou esteem'st the ornament of life / And live a coward in thine own esteem, letting 'I dare not' wait upon 'I would' ...?" (I.vii.41–3) she asks him. And following this first murder (of Duncan, the king), when Macbeth begins to show compunctions or guilt feelings about what he has done, she shames him explicitly with the taunt: "My hands are of your color [red, bloody]; but I shame / To wear a heart so white" (II.ii. 61–2). Later, when Macbeth hallucinates Banquo's

[6] Gilligan and Richards (2009); Gilligan and Richards (2018).   [7] Gilligan (2011).
[8] Fenichel (1945), p. 139.   [9] Ibid., p. 493.

ghost after having arranged for his murder, Lady Macbeth shames him again by directly questioning his adequacy as a man:

> Are you a man?
> ... these flaws and starts ... would well become
> A woman's story at a winter's fire,
> Authorized by her grandam. Shame itself
> Why do you make such faces?
> ... What? quite unmann'd in folly?
> ... Fie, for shame!
>
> (III.iv.55–73)

And Macbeth gets the message. As he says later in that same conversation, "If trembling I inhabit then, protest me / The baby of a girl" – or, in other words, if the body I inhabit trembles with fear, proclaim me a baby girl (III.iv.104–5).

Shakespeare's perception here of the demands placed on Macbeth could hardly be more astute, for as he sees, it is only by killing Duncan and subsequently Banquo and the family of Macduff that he can avoid shame and achieve honor, satisfy his ambition (and the ambitions of his wife for both of them), and by doing so prove that he is a man (rather than a coward or a woman).

However, as the tragedy unfolds, it also becomes clear why this strategy for living is as self-defeating as drinking salt water to quench a thirst. At the simplest and most concrete level, violence provokes retaliatory violence. But it also fails to achieve the psychological goal that is the reason for shame's existence and the function it serves in promoting psychological growth or health, namely, to motivate people to mature, to gain or develop the skills and abilities, the knowledge and competencies which will enable them to help both themselves and others.

To the extent that people achieve these goals, they are much less likely to experience a need or wish to harm others or themselves, or make others feel inferior to them. Working with violent men in prisons and jails, I (James Gilligan) have witnessed the remarkable consistency with which violent men abandon violence as their default means of warding off shame and achieving pride once nonviolent means of achieving self-esteem, self-respect, and feelings of self-worth, such as education, become available to them.

Shame motivates people to become active in their pursuit of strength, skills, and knowledge and thus to gain the pride that results from these achievements. However, when one lives in a social or political environment or culture that is a hierarchical, inegalitarian, and authoritarian shame culture, that is, an environment that places roadblocks in the way of a man's ability to achieve pride and self-esteem and thus reinforces his feeling that he is inferior to other people in whatever respects are important to him, no matter how energetically and strenuously he may have sought to overcome these impediments, he eventually becomes exhausted, depleted by the constant pressure to be active, aggressive, dominant, self-reliant, risk-taking, and violent in order to be perceived as a man. When people have reached this point, death – and especially violent death – may appear as the only way they can rest without losing face, that is, without being shamed for being "passive" or weak.

This observation illuminates what otherwise may appear inexplicable: the state that both Macbeth and Lady Macbeth ultimately reach, along with the murderers they hire. As the first murderer expresses it, he is "So *weary* with disasters, tugg'd with fortune, / That I would set my life on any chance. / To mend it, or *be rid on't*" (III.i.110–13, emphases added). And not long after the murderer makes his confession of world-weariness, Macbeth makes the same point even more explicitly:

> Better be with the dead,
> Whom we, to gain our peace, have sent to peace,
> Than on the torture of the mind to lie
> In restless ecstasy [a frenzy of agitation]. Duncan is in his grave,
> After life's fitful fever he sleeps well.
> Treason has done his worst; nor steel, nor poison,
> Malice domestic, foreign levy, nothing,
> Can touch him further.
>
> (III.ii.19–26).

This same dynamic plays out among violent men in prison. For them, the only face-saving, "masculine" way they can allow themselves to rest and be passive (rather than violent and active) is to behave in a way they know will send them to prison – where they can disguise the wish to rest and be cared for behind the mask of machismo and hypermasculinity. They can pretend or even lie to themselves that the only reason they are not active most of the time (violent or actively pursuing goals of dominance or self-aggrandizement) is because they are in a place (a prison) that forces them to be inactive – especially if they are so violent that they are placed in solitary confinement. But when even that is not enough, they will say, much in the manner of Macbeth, how their goal in life is to go to their own death in a hail of gunfire, though only after they have killed as many other people as possible before they themselves are killed by the police.

In this way, they can disguise the wish to become dead, but only in a face-saving way, making their death a consequence of their being so active and aggressive rather than because they, like Macbeth, envy the dead who are at last able to "rest in peace." Or, as Macbeth himself puts it earlier in the play, "I am in blood / Stepp'd in so far that, should I wade no more, / Returning were as tedious as to go o'er" (III.iv.135–7).

CHAPTER 6

Moral Nihilism and the Paralysis of Action:
Hamlet *and* Troilus and Cressida

Shakespeare virtually begs us to understand his play *Hamlet* in the same terms that Hamlet asks his actors and audience to understand *his* play, "The Mouse-Trap." He explains that "the purpose of playing" is to engage in an activity "whose end, both at the first and now, was and is, to hold as 'twere, the mirror up to nature; to show ... the very age and body of the time his form and pressure" (III.ii.23–7). In these terms, Hamlet (the character) can be seen as the first modern personality, because in Shakespeare's tragedy Hamlet confronts head-on the "form and pressure" of Shakespeare's time, namely, the collapse of the medieval worldview and the transition to the modern scientific mentality.

The scientific revolution was conceived in the sixteenth century by Copernicus and was born in the seventeenth century, beginning with Galileo (who was born in the same year as Shakespeare). As Hamlet sees, a major implication of this shift in consciousness from the world of ghosts and witches to the world of science, in which knowledge is based on empirical evidence, was a loss of faith in the credibility of moral values and commandments, which are derived not from evidence but from pure (and hence subjective and arbitrary) reason. As he put it, "There is nothing either good or bad but thinking makes it so." (II.ii.250–51)

With this, Hamlet sums up his dilemma. He does not, and even cannot, know what he *should* do. Throughout the play, he continues to ask, "What should we do?" (I.iv.57), and his mother is equally clueless as to what her moral obligations are: "What shall I do?" (III.iv.180). He pleads with his father, to no avail, "Let me not burst in ignorance" (I.iv.46). And well toward the end of the play, he is still lamenting this lack of knowledge: "I do not know / Why yet I live to say, 'This thing's to do" (IV.iv.43–4).

In part, this is because two opposing moral value systems are in play: the shame ethic exemplified by the Ghost, Hamlet's father, whose commandment is "Thou shalt kill," and the guilt ethics at the center of the moral teachings of Christianity, which were ostensibly the official moral value system of that time, which give the opposite commandment, namely, "Thou shalt not kill." By the end of the play, Hamlet has managed to become both a perpetrator and a victim of murder, but in a chaotic, disorganized, largely accidental, and barely purposeful manner. This is consistent with, and a result of, the anomie or moral nihilism caused by his inability to believe in either of the two opposite and antagonistic moral value systems, and to decide that either one is more truthful and hence believable and credible than the other one in establishing what is good and evil. Nor is he able to find some other basis, besides a moral one, for making decisions as to what to do.

In our analysis of shame and guilt ethics and their effects on the major protagonists of Shakespeare's history plays and tragedies, we have stressed the centrality of the moral emotions and their corresponding value systems. Here, to "pluck out the heart of [Hamlet's] mystery," it is necessary to shift our focus, recognizing that Hamlet's central conflict – and one unique to his major problem in living, his inability to make up his mind as to what he should do – is not simply an emotional conflict, it is also – and primarily – a cognitive conflict. Hamlet expresses this in many different ways throughout the play, including the above quoted line – "there is nothing either good or bad but thinking makes it so." Thus Hamlet conveys his awareness of the subjectivity of moral value judgments, his perception that judgments of good and bad are constructions of the mind (i.e., of thought) rather than objective facts or realities. In the tragedy of *Hamlet*, Shakespeare shows us the breakdown of both the cosmological and the moral hierarchies that had dominated Christendom for so long.

As John Donne, Shakespeare's contemporary, expressed it: "The new Philosophy calls all in doubt ..., 'Tis all in pieces, all coherence gone." And his slightly older contemporary, Montaigne (with whose work Shakespeare was very familiar), said the same thing: "To philosophize is to doubt." The "philosophizing" they were both referring to was more specifically what we now call "science" – a word (from the Latin for "knowledge") that was not used in its modern sense until the nineteenth century. For science, unlike the faith-based world of medieval culture, is based on doubt; its motto might well be "take nothing on faith: believe only in those hypotheses that have been confirmed, and not yet disconfirmed, by empirical data" – that is, facts that are observable and testable by everyone, not subjective opinions exclusive to one person alone, or dogmas pronounced by past authorities. Moral hypotheses, however, are unable to meet these criteria and thus can express only opinions, not knowledge. This is what Donne described when he wrote, "There's nothing simply good, nor ill alone, / Of every quality comparison / The only measure is, and judge Opinion."[1] Or as Montaigne put it, "the taste of goods or evils doth greatly depend on the opinion we have of them." And "if it is from ourselves [i.e., from our own thoughts, feelings, and opinions alone] that we derive the ruling of our conduct, into what confusion do we cast ourselves!"[2] Hamlet's statement that good and bad are nothing more than our own thoughts is virtually a paraphrase of that last quotation.

In *Hamlet*, then, Shakespeare, "the soul of his age," as Ben Jonson called him, shows us not only how inescapable moral skepticism and agnosticism were at the time in which he was living and writing, but also, in excruciating detail, how disorganizing and ultimately fatal it is to experience a cognitive vacuum in the realm of practical reason. With his character Hamlet, Shakespeare dramatizes the mental incoherence and chaos and the behavioral paralysis that follows from having no way of knowing what to do (on the basis of moral value systems). All of which was one of the dangerous by-products of the advances being made in the sphere of speculative reason, by the modern natural sciences.

Hamlet's indecision, his vacillation and paralysis of action, are far more deadly for everyone involved (most of whom had nothing to do with harming Hamlet's father or anyone else) than would have been the case had he recognized that he was faced with a problem that in the social, legal, and political circumstances of his time he simply did not have the ability or power or knowledge to solve, and had instead mourned his father's death (since even revenge would not undo the murder and bring his father back to life), and returned to Wittenberg to complete his studies.

As it is, Hamlet becomes caught in the paralysis of nihilism. He is faced with two questions, each of which he finds it difficult to answer. The first is: Did his uncle kill his father? The second is: If Claudius did kill his father, what should Hamlet do about it? But these questions are quite different. The first is an empirical question, to which a truthful answer can (in principle) be found by means of evidence, or data. The second is a moral question, to which there is no apparent basis for deciding whether any given answer is truthful (i.e., expressive of knowledge).

Hamlet's approach to answering the first question is to abandon the medieval worldview – believing in (or taking on faith) the reality of ghosts returning from the dead – and pursue instead a scientific, empirical method of inquiry. In doing this, he anticipates modern psychological

---

[1] Donne (1611), pp. 206–42.   [2] Montaigne (1965).

science by devising an ingenious social-psychological experiment, called here a "play within a play." By means of this experiment (remember, Shakespeare is the modern world's first – and also greatest – psychologist) he will test the king's guilt or innocence by seeking empirical evidence (which is more trustworthy than the words of a ghost, of whose nature, reality, and truthfulness he cannot be sure). Thus, "The play's the thing, / Wherein I'll catch the conscience of the king" (II.ii.633–4). Not the unprovable assertions of a ghost, but rather, a scientific experiment designed to elicit a psychological reaction which he can observe for himself.

However, no empirical test can answer his *moral* question, namely, What should he do? Follow the commandments of his father's shame ethic and undo the dishonor his father suffered by committing an honor-killing, thus avenging the murder and cuckolding of his father (as if that would magically undo the past – the murder, the dishonor)? Or engage in one of the alternatives suggested by guilt ethics, namely, kill himself as a means of diverting his hostility toward his uncle against himself? Or, as a third alternative, follow the path laid out in the Sermon on the Mount, and transcend morality altogether: resist not evil, love and forgive your enemies, and kill no one? But Hamlet makes it clear, in his speeches to Ophelia and elsewhere, that he is no longer capable of loving anyone, himself or others.

Without a means for answering these questions, Hamlet – and everyone else so afflicted – finds it difficult if not impossible to have a basis for making decisions and acting, just as walking in quicksand makes locomotion impossible. Confronting a vacuum in the sphere of practical reason (and human nature hates a cognitive vacuum), Hamlet finds himself in an untenable and unviable mental condition, namely, moral nihilism – a condition that is incompatible with ongoing life, which constantly requires us to make decisions as to how we are going to regulate our relationships with other people, and also with ourselves: to have sufficient self-love, and freedom from self-hate, to go on taking care of ourselves, as well as of others.

In dramatizing the paralysis caused by moral nihilism, *Hamlet* stands apart from all the other tragedies as well as the history plays in Shakespeare's canon (although another play written at almost the same time, *Troilus and Cressida,* does raise enough of the same issues, albeit on a much smaller scale, that we will discuss it as well in this chapter). For while all the other plays can be interpreted as dramatizing the conflict between shame and guilt, and between shame and guilt ethics, *Hamlet* is unique in that in it Shakespeare shows us the catastrophe that occurs when *both* moral value systems – shame ethics *and* guilt ethics – have lost their credibility. Or rather, are equally credible, since they are diametrical opposites and cancel each other out, which renders each of them equally noncredible. And since he cannot find any credible basis for deciding which of these ethics to choose, Hamlet is left with no criteria in which he can believe for deciding how to act. The sheer number and length of his soliloquies suggests the depth of his mental anguish over this quandary.

Moral nihilism refers to the inability to find any credible answers to the questions raised by the sphere in our thinking that philosophers from Aristotle to Kant have called practical reason, namely, questions of how to live and what to do – questions to which moral belief systems claim to have answers. Without criteria in which he can believe for answering these questions and making decisions about how to act, Hamlet is paralyzed into indecision.

This does not mean that he does not feel plenty of both shame and guilt. Clearly, he is extraordinarily sensitive to both moral emotions. In one of the most impassioned self-accusations of his own guilt in any of Shakespeare's plays (with the possible exception of Othello's self-laceration over his murder of Desdemona), but without even having committed any major sins in reality (as far as we are told), Hamlet gives the following judgment of himself, condemning himself in the terms of guilt ethics with its repudiation of pride, ambition, revenge, and aggression when he says:

> I am myself indifferent honest; but yet I could accuse me of such things that it were better my mother had not borne me: I am very proud, revengeful, ambitious, with more offences at my beck than I have thoughts to put them in, imagination to give them shape, or time to act them in. What should such fellows as I do, crawling between earth and heaven? (III.i.123–30)

Yet just before saying this about himself, he says it is true of all men, telling Ophelia, "Get thee to a nunnery: why wouldst thou be a breeder of sinners?" (III.i.122–3). And the degree to which he feels that he, and all men, are guilty and deserve punishment (i.e., the doctrine of original sin or universal sinfulness) is reflected in the severity of his moral condemnation of himself and everyone else: "Use every man according to his desert and who should 'scape whipping?" (II.ii.561). This speech in fact is a paraphrase of Psalm 129, "Out of the depths I cry unto thee, O Lord ... If thou dids't keep account of offenses, O Lord, who would endure it?"

When Rosencrantz tells him, "the world's grown honest," he cannot believe it. He replies, "Then is doomsday near; but our news is not true."

In another expression of his moral accusation against people in general, he says, "to be honest, as this world goes, is to be one man picked out of ten thousand" (II.ii.179). In fact, this is at least a partial paraphrase of what Jesus said about the universality of sin and guilt: "Let him who is without sin cast the first stone" – a sentiment that inhibits not only honor killings in general, but also Hamlet's specific obligation to avenge his father's dishonor, and thus restore it, by murdering Claudius. As he says to Ophelia: "We are errant knaves, all: believe none of us" (III.i.130). All of these statements are consistent with the notion that everyone, including himself, is a sinner who is in need of forgiveness, so that he has no right to punish other sinners – and not only because doing so would be the height of hypocrisy. In fact, as different as the two texts are, *Hamlet* is virtually identical to the New Testament in the frequency with which Hamlet insists that all men are sinners, all men are guilty (and, for that matter, so are all women).

However, Hamlet also judges himself by the opposite values of shame ethics, with its contempt toward cowardice, submitting to oppression rather than eliminating it, and resorting to words rather than violence, and as a result despises himself as a coward, an ass, and a (male) whore. "Am I a coward?. . . Who calls me villain?. . . I am pigeon-liver'd and lack gall. . . . To make oppression bitter . . . Why, what an ass I am! This is most brave, . . . That I, . . . Must like a whore, unpack my heart with words" (II.ii.593ff.).

He then blames his shamefulness (his cowardice and passivity) on his guilt-inflicting conscience. What his guilt feelings motivate him to do (forgive and forget) is valued negatively by his feelings of shame, which motivate him to hate his uncle and murder him. Thus his guilt-motivated inhibition of violence toward Claudius, and his preference for words, dialogue, and reason rather than violent action (both of which are virtues, according to guilt ethics), are reconstructed as cowardice (a vice, according to shame ethics), which exposes Hamlet to the self-accusation of being a coward:

> Thus conscience [the source of guilt feelings] does make cowards of us all;
> And thus the native hue of resolution
> Is sicklied o'er with the pale cast of thought,
> And enterprises of great pitch and moment
> With this regard their currents turn awry,
> And lose the name of action.
>
> (III.i.82–7)

Throughout the play, Hamlet is torn in two opposite directions: between the obligation to commit murder, which his father's shame ethic commands him to do as his filial duty, and his own self-motivated temptation to commit what his guilty conscience demands of him instead, namely, the exactly opposite behavior, suicide. It is not merely that he continues to vacillate between believing and doubting the ghost's authenticity – though he certainly does do that. In fact, he laments throughout most of the play that "The spirit I have seen / May be a devil – and the devil hath power / T'assume a pleasing shape" (II.ii.551–3) and "Observe my uncle; if his occulted guilt / Do not itself unkennel in one speech, / It is a damned ghost that we have seen, / And my imaginations are as foul / As Vulcan's stithy" (III.ii.80–4).

So Hamlet does doubt the ghost's authenticity and honesty, and thus continues to be uncertain of Claudius's guilt and his mother's infidelity until the play within the play resolves his doubts about those matters. But even when he finally comes to believe that his father's ghost had spoken the truth about the facts in question, he is still unable to organize his behavior around any coherent set of values, that is, any morally motivated and morally comprehensible purpose, either of revenge (homicide) or of suicide – both of which he stumbles into more by accident than by design. Even the sword with which he stabs Claudius comes into his hands by accident (in the course of his duel with Laertes), and both his and his mother's deaths are just as accidental.

For Hamlet's deeper problem – the deeper cause of his inability to make any clear decisions as to what to do – is not simply an emotional one. Hamlet is sensitive to both shame and guilt, and they impel opposite behaviors, so that, caught between these two opposing affects he is rendered paralyzed. But almost everyone is vulnerable and sensitive to both shame and guilt at one time and to one degree or another, and yet is motivated to act by whichever is the stronger emotion in any given situation. The deeper cause of Hamlet's indecision and passivity is a cognitive one: his inability to discover any way to know what he should do and how he ought to live (and die). What Shakespeare dramatizes as Hamlet's tragedy is his inability to find any set of moral values or principles in which he can believe, and on the basis of which he could answer these questions.

It is in his conversation with Rosencranz that Hamlet makes what we have highlighted as the ultimate statement of his moral perplexity. Having said that "Denmark's a prison," to which Rosencrantz replies, "We think not so, my lord," Hamlet then says, "Why then 'tis none to you; for *there is nothing either good or bad but thinking makes it so*" (II.ii.246–7, emphasis added). What's more, Hamlet was quite right in saying, "The time is out of joint: O cursed spite, that ever I was born to set it right" (I.v.189–90). Shakespeare created his character Hamlet at exactly the point of transition from the medieval to the modern worldview – the time when science had, as Donne observed, called into doubt every nonempirical way of thinking, including moral thinking, but had not yet come up with any credible replacement or substitute for thinking about behavior in terms of morality. More specifically, Hamlet existed at a time in the history of Western civilization – the time of the scientific revolution – which resulted in the death not only of God (and his counterpart and antagonist, the devil) – but also of good and evil, the abstractions of which God and the devil are the mythological personifications, but at which time no credible alternative to moral ways of thinking had yet been created.

Unable to believe in either a guilt ethic or a shame ethic, Hamlet is not immoral; he is amoral, or morally agnostic, meaning that he is suffering behavioral paralysis because he has lost the ability to believe in the validity of either of the two opposite moral value systems – which leaves him incapable of answering the questions of practical reason, namely, how to live and what to do. And this cognitive vacuum in the sphere of practical reason is what we mean by moral nihilism.

Moral nihilism is also at the center of *Troilus and Cressida*, which is among the reasons Anne Barton is correct in describing it as "closely associated" with *Hamlet*. For like *Hamlet, Troilus* is "the presentation of a society in which fixed or objective values no longer operate." Pointing to "the stubborn relativism of the work," she points out that although "Ulysses' speech on degree in I.iii. has long been regarded as the corner-stone of the 'Elizabethan world-picture,' evidence of Shakespeare's funda-mental conservatism," when "Looked at in context, . . . this speech reveals itself as an adroit stringing together of pious platitudes . . . which is applauded by all but to which no one, least of all Ulysses himself, pays the smallest practical attention." This is rather like Polonius' speech to Laertes (I.iii.57–80), we would add, which served an equivalent purpose in *Hamlet* – as an ironic parody of conventional but meaningless moral platitudes that have lost their relevance and credibility. Barton continues that "absolutes of good or evil are grotesquely out of place" in the world of *Troilus*. Thus, "the play is a brilliant but scarifying vision of a world in pieces, all value and coherence gone . . . the picture of man which it presents is pessimistic almost to the point of nihilism." Thus, "*Troilus and Cressida* moves toward a position of profound skepticism. The play . . . finishes by portraying a chaos which can no longer be remedied by traditional means. Accepted ideas of degree and rule, of personal honor, reputation and love, do not, in this society, require reaffirmation so much as radical redefinition." This is a play that Shakespeare has used to "describe a world whose values are not stable, a world of chaos and relativity."[3]

In the Prologue (30–1), Shakespeare sets the stage: "Like or find fault, do as your pleasures are, Now good or bad, 'tis but the chance of war." In what follows, good and bad are in fact as arbitrary as chance. Troilus comments sardonically, "Fools on both sides! Helen must needs be fair / When with your blood you daily paint her thus" (I.i.90–1).

This is a world in which value (including moral value) is, as Anne Barton observes, "a function of the law of supply and demand."[4] In her first conversation concerning Troilus' declaration of love for her, Cressida uses market terms to explain her reluctance to acknowledge her love for him, noting that "Men prize the thing ungain'd more than it is" (I.ii.289).

But the most comprehensive deconstruction of morality is presented ironically, paradoxically, and therefore much more powerfully, by Ulysses in his speech, the intention of which is to defend moral order (including what in today's political rhetoric might be described as "law and order"). In seeking to explain why the Greeks have not yet conquered Troy, Ulysses contends that it is because "The specialty of rule hath been neglected" – that is, some of their most capable soldiers such as Achilles have not respected and obeyed the orders of their superiors, in this case Agamemnon. Ulysses then goes on to say that "Degree" (by which he means rank and authority in the political/military hierarchy) "being vizarded," or masked and thus not recognized or respected, "Th' unworthiest shows as fairly," or is valued as highly as those who are actually or objectively of higher worth. And indeed, Ulysses believes that the necessity for dividing the human world into the superior and the inferior is demonstrated by the natural world, which in his belief, does the same thing. Yet as Ulysses elaborates his worldview, it becomes clear that the universe he is describing is not the world of modern science which had replaced astrology with astronomy, nor the world of Copernicus with its heliocentric solar system, but rather the prescientific universe of Ptolemy with the earth (not the sun) at its center:

> The heavens themselves, the planets, and this centre [the earth]
> Observe degree, priority and place,
> Insisture, course, proportion, season, form,

---

[3] Barton (1974), pp. 443–7.   [4] Ibid.

Office, and custom, in all line of order . . .
. . . but when the planets
In evil mixture to disorder wander,
What plagues and what portents, what mutiny! What raging of the sea,
    shaking of earth!
. . . O, when degree is shak'd,
Which is the ladder of all high designs,
The enterprise is sick . . .
Take but degree away, untune that string,
And hark what discord follows. Each thing meets
In mere oppugnancy . . .
Strength should be lord of imbecility [weakness],
And the rude son should strike his father dead;
Force should be right, or rather *right and wrong*
(Between whose endless jar justice resides)
Should lose their names, and so should justice too!

> (I.ii.78–118; emphasis added)

Here Ulysses predicts what did happen when the modern scientific
mentality replaced the more credulous and hierarchical mindset of the
Middle Ages. Traditional religious, moral, and political verities (right and
wrong, justice and injustice) lost their credibility. In *Troilus and Cressida* as
in *Hamlet,* Shakespeare shows us the origins (and the consequences) of the
cognitive vacuum created by what Nietzsche called the "death" of God and
morality. Since Shakespeare's time, many have agreed with Ulysses that if
hierarchy along with social and political inequality were challenged or
overthrown, chaos would follow. Hence the need, as an alternative or
antidote to nihilism, for an all-powerful, infallible leader or savior, vari-
ously called Fuhrer, Duce, Ayatollah, "Big Brother," "dear Leader," and so
forth. As Ulysses put it, without a clear moral, social, and political
hierarchy, dividing people into the superior and the inferior,

> . . . everything [would] include itself in power,
> Power into will, will into appetite,
> And appetite, an universal wolf
> (So double seconded with will and power),
> Must make perforce an universal prey,
> And last eat up himself. Great Agamemnon,
> This chaos, when degree is suffocate[d]
> Follows the choking . . .
>
> (I.ii.119–26)

But Troilus continues to point out the subjectivity of values. When
Hector says of Helen, the cause of the catastrophic war they were still

fighting, "she is not worth what she doth cost the keeping," Troilus replies, "*What's aught, save as 'tis valued?*" (emphasis added). This scandalizes Hector, who insists,

> But value dwells not in particular will,
> It holds his estimate and dignity
> As well wherein 'tis precious of itself
> As in the prizer.
>
> (II.ii.51–6)

This discussion of the subjectivity of values continues when Ajax challenges Achilles' claim to martial superiority over all other Greek warriors: "What is he more than another?" Ajax asks. To which Agamemnon replies, "No more than what he thinks he is" (II.iii.142–3) As Anne Barton's editorial note in *The Riverside Shakespeare* paraphrases this, "his worth lies only in his self-estimation."[5]

The point is addressed again when Ulysses says, "Imagin'd worth / Holds in his blood" (II.iii.172–3). But this raises the question (which seems already to have been answered in the play): Is there any other kind of worth except "Imagin'd"?

Agamemnon offers a devastating analysis of the psychological causes and consequences of this kind of imagined superiority to others: "He that is proud eats up himself. Pride is his own glass, his own trumpet, his own chronicle, and whatever praises itself but in the deed [in any way except by silently doing the deed], devours the deed in the praise" (II.iii.154–7).

Shakespeare's final demonstration of the absence of any firm belief in moral values in the world he brings to life in this play occurs when Paris refuses to end the war by returning Helen to Menelaus. Hector then objects on the grounds that doing so would violate moral law and bring "Disgrace to your great worths, and shame to me," even though his oracular sister Cassandra has already prophesied, "Troy burns, or else let Helen go" (II.ii.112):

> Paris and Troilus, you have both said well,
> ... but superficially, not much
> Unlike young men, whom Aristotle thought
> Unfit to hear moral philosophy.
> The reasons you allege do more conduce
> To the hot passion of distemper'd blood,
> Than to make up a free determination

5 Ibid.

> 'Twixt right and wrong; for pleasure and revenge
> Have ears more deaf than adders to the voice
> Of any true decision. Nature craves
> All dues be render'd to their owners; now,
> What nearer debt in all humanity
> Than wife is to the husband? If this law
> Of nature be corrupted through affection . . .
> There is a law in each well order'd nation
> To curb those raging appetites . . .
> If Helen then be wife to Sparta's king,
> As is known she is, these moral laws
> Of nature and of nations speak aloud
> To have her back return'd. Thus to persist
> In doing wrong extenuates not wrong,
> But makes it much more heavy. Hector's opinion
> Is this in the way of truth.

Nevertheless, even though Hector here expresses a firm belief in what true morality (natural law, Aristotelian ethics) commands, as opposed to affection, pleasure, and revenge, he goes on to completely contradict himself and simply abandon what he has just claimed as his opinion as to what the moral law requires:

> . . . yet ne'er the less . . .
> I propend to you . . . to keep Helen still,
> For 'tis a cause that hath no mean dependence
> Upon our joint and several dignities.

In short, despite his clear and firm statement of what morality (what we call a guilt morality) would require, Hector agrees with Paris (and Troilus) that it is better to keep fighting, no matter the risk that doing so will cause Troy to burn, than for the men in the city-state to suffer indignity and shame. As Troilus puts it, immediately after Hector's speech,

> . . . worthy Hector,
> She is a theme of honor and renown,
> A spur to valiant and magnanimous deeds,
> Whose present courage may beat down our foes,
> And fame in time to come canonize us.
>
> (II.ii.163–202)

Hector had just spoken as if guilt ethics (such as Aristotle's) were valid, but then immediately chose to follow his desire for pride and honor because following the guilt ethic would expose him to feelings of shame, indignity, and dishonor. But he does not speak as if he were defending a shame ethic in which he can claim to believe – for he has already declared the validity of "the moral laws of nature and of nations," which he has just described as prescribing behavior that is the opposite of that demanded by their "dignities" (i.e., their honor and pride). Instead, he is letting his behavior be determined by the emotional need to avoid the painful feelings of shame and the consequent loss of dignity and to achieve the pleasurable emotions of pride and dignity, or self-worth. The fact that guilt ethics is no sooner evoked than it is abandoned (in order to avoid shame and disgrace) makes it clear that even he is acting on the basis of his subjective feelings rather than a set of moral values or principles in whose truth or validity or even rationality he can believe.

Ulysses, in contrast, does describe a firm and orderly set of reasons for believing in and upholding the shame ethic that he described earlier in the play – albeit an ethical code so saturated in a no longer credible prescientific worldview that it loses its credibility (to the audience). All that Hector appeals to in his speech is the fact that he has moral emotions – shame versus honor – but he gives no indication of having organized these feelings into a coherent moral value system or cognitive structure in which he can believe.

And lest it appear that Shakespeare in this play is quietly defending the shame/honor ethic that the Trojans (like the Greeks) have embraced and for which they are fighting the war, he has Thersites (in the Greek camp) ridicule and denounce the absurdity of war and the reasons for it immediately after Hector's speech. Denouncing the "little little less than little wit" that the main warriors on his side (Ajax and Achilles) have and "The common curse of mankind, folly and ignorance" (II.iii.28), Thersites calls for "the curse depending [falling] on those that war for a placket" (a slang term for a woman). Thus he puts the war in perspective, a war that has gone on for eight years, saying, "All the argument is a whore and a cuckold, a good quarrel to draw emulous [ridiculous] factions and bleed to death upon.... war and lechery confound all!" (II.iii.72–5). Hardly a matter of dignity, knowledge, rationality, or morality!

This becomes even clearer with Troilus, the most Hamlet-like character in the play. Despite having earlier endorsed Paris and Hector's decision to fight the war for the sake of honor, he experiences a shock that renders him unable to believe in any coherent sense of morality or reality, whether based on shame or guilt, when he sees Cressida betraying him with a liaison with the Greek warrior Diomedes. While Troilus claims that his refusal to believe in what he has just seen "hath no taste of madness" (V.ii.127), he suffers a breakdown in both spheres of his thinking: his speculative reason, which assesses reality, and his practical reason, which assesses morality. Cressida's betrayal, after her promises of fidelity, has robbed him of the belief that morality was anything more than "words, words, words ... words and errors," (V.ii.108–11), in an echo of Hamlet's similar lament. And like Hamlet, Troilus becomes suicidal: "I reck [care] not that I end my life today" (V.vi.26).

Not only has Cressida destroyed Troilus' capacity to believe that morality still has meaning, reality, credibility, or validity, Achilles also has demonstrated the death of the moral code based on shame, which demands that violence be practiced in a courageous manner, not a cowardly one. For Achilles killed Hector when he happened upon him at a time when Hector had just taken off his armor and laid down his sword, not when Hector was fighting him as an equal, able to defend himself. Yet despite having killed an unarmed man – a serious violation of the code of honor of shame ethics, which requires that you exhibit courage, and thus gain honor, by fighting only those of equal power – he boasts, "Achilles hath the mighty Hector slain!" (V.viii.14).

Troilus ends the play by vowing to revenge the dishonorable way in which Achilles killed Hector, but he does so not for any moral reason but purely as a way of assuaging the emotional pain and shame he feels over Cressida's sexual infidelity to him. As he says, "Hope of revenge" against Achilles "shall hide our inward woe" over Cressida's betrayal (V.x.31). For Troilus, morality, including shame ethics, is dead, so the best he can hope for is to make violent behavior serve the purpose of emotional anesthesia, if not a means of committing suicide vicariously – again, much like Hamlet.

CHAPTER 7

Apocalyptic Violence
Timon of Athens

In *Othello* and *Macbeth*, Shakespeare showed how shame and shame ethics can motivate homicide and how guilt and guilt ethics can motivate suicide. In both of these plays, the major protagonists – Othello and Macbeth – remained committed to one or (at different times) both of those moral emotions and value systems, acted on them, and ultimately died because of them. In both plays, the violence was directed at specific individuals, for a specific purpose, and in that sense displayed some sense of recognizable and comprehensible order, though in Macbeth's case the violence did become, by the end, increasingly without limits and desperate. Yet at least the violence against others had a recognizable purpose: to achieve honor, in the sense either of regaining lost honor (Othello) or of preventing the loss of honor and gaining a new honor and then fighting to keep it (Macbeth).

In contrast, *Timon of Athens* dramatizes what we are calling apocalyptic violence: the most unlimited violence in which humans can engage. In this pattern of violence, the major characters are so consumed with the desire for revenge that they want to bring about the apocalypse: the death of everyone, the entire human world, including themselves. Like Samson in the Bible, they are enraged to the point of wanting to bring the roof down on the heads of their enemies – and they see everyone around them as enemies – in a universal bloodbath from which no one will escape, including themselves.

Shakespeare's Timon is a man of considerable wealth, presumably the result of a successful military career; as a younger man, he saved Athens from its enemies. By the time the play begins, his main purpose in life has come to consist in giving lavish dinner parties and gifts of money or objects of value to his friends and acquaintances, whether they need them or not (though some genuinely do: one, in order to escape from debtors' prison, and another, to marry a rich man's daughter). Timon does not worry whether he can actually afford to be so generous, for as he says to his friends, "the gods themselves have provided that I shall have much help from you: how had you been my friends else? . . . what need we have any friends, if we should ne'er have need of 'em?" (I.ii.88–90, 95–6). And in what proves an especially ironic comment, which he will later come to regret: 'I have often wish'd myself poorer, that I might come nearer to you. We are born to do benefits; and what better or properer can we call our own than the riches of our friends? O, what a precious comfort 'tis, to have so many like brothers commanding one another's fortunes" (I.ii.100–5).

When his steward Flavius informs him that he has been too prodigal with his wealth and now has debts coming due that are greater than his assets, Timon acknowledges his error, but then rationalizes it, saying, "No villainous bounty yet hath pass'd my heart; Unwisely, not ignobly, have I given" (I.ii.173–4) He then comforts himself with the thought that "I am wealthy in my friends" (I.ii.184).

However, he soon learns that none of the friends toward whom he has been so generous, and who flattered him ostentatiously when he was showering them with his gifts, was willing to loan him any money of their own with which to repay his debts. Flavius comments that "when the means are gone that buy this praise, The breath is gone whereof this praise is made. Feast-won, fast-lost" (I.ii.169–71).

This is the point where Timon loses his faith in humanity, his generosity, and his love toward other people. One of the major ironies in the play is that here Timon finally reaches the same conclusions that Apemantus, "a churlish philosopher," had been warning him about from the beginning of the play, but which he, Timon, had previously refused to listen to, such as, "I wonder men dare trust themselves with men" (I.ii.43). And "Who lives that's not depraved or depraves? Who dies that bears not one spurn [blow, injury] to their graves / Of their friends' gift?" (I.ii.140–2). And speaking of Timon's refusal to listen to what both he (Apemantus) and Flavius were trying to warn him of, Apemantus says, "O that men's ears should be / To counsel deaf, but not to flattery?" (I.ii. 249–50).

A further irony is that Timon's blindness – his initial "tragic flaw" – was his moral rectitude. As Lucullus, one of the flattering lords who is refusing to help him, puts it: "Every man has his fault, and honesty is his" (III.i.27–8). Or as Flavius describes him,

> Poor honest lord, brought low by his own heart,
> Undone by goodness! Strange, unusual blood,
> When man's worst sin is, he does too much good!
> Who then dares to be half so kind again?
> For bounty, that makes gods, do still mar men.
>
> (IV.ii.37–41)

Timon is so shocked by the disloyalty of those whom he had thought were his friends that he decides to isolate himself from all other human beings and to live by himself in "the woods, where he shall find Th' unkindest beast more kinder than mankind" (IV.i.36–7). He declares, "I am sick of this false world.... Then, Timon, ... prepare thy grave" (IV.iii.37). He exemplifies what we have already described as the "death of the self" that people experience when they feel irreversibly and incurably humiliated: he already feels dead psychologically, as a person, so his last remaining wish, before he dies physically as well, is to revenge himself against the world by bringing everyone else down into death with him. He composes an epitaph for his grave that describes the state he has already reached, emotionally and psychologically: "Timon is dead.... Some beast read this: there does not live a man" (i.e., all men are beasts: there are no men, only beasts – but also, I am dead, and so is everyone else) (V.iii.3–4).

So Timon renounces his faith in both morality and humanity: "Burn house! Sink Athens! Henceforth hated be, Of Timon, man and all humanity!" (III.vi.104–5). Continuing in this vein, he elaborates his desires:

> Bankrupts, hold fast;
> Rather than render back, out with your knives,
> And cut your trusters' [creditors] throats!
> ... Son of sixteen,
> Pluck the lin'd crutch from thy old limping sire,
> With it beat out his brains!
>
> (IV.I.8–13)

He not only wants all humans to die; he wants morality to do the same: "Piety, and fear, Religion [reverence] to the gods, peace, justice, truth, ... Degrees, observances, customs, and laws, Decline to your confounding contraries [i.e., turn into your opposites, thus producing chaos and utter ruin]; And yet confusion live!" (i.e., let nothing but chaos and destruction, of humanity and morality, continue) (IV.i.15–21).

> Plagues ...
> Your potent and infectious fevers heap
> On Athens ...
> Lust, and liberty,
> Creep in the minds and marrows of our youth,
> That 'gainst the streams of virtue they may strive,
> And drown themselves in riot!...
> The gods confound (hear me, you good gods all)
> Th' Athenians, both within and out that wall!
> And grant, as Timon grows, his hate may grow

> To the whole race of mankind, high and low!
> Amen.
>
> (IV.i.21–41)

He concludes then:

> There's nothing level in our cursed natures
> But direct villainy. Therefore be abhorr'd
> All feasts, societies, and throngs of men!...
> Destruction fang mankind!
>
> (IV.iii.19–23)

When he discovers a cache of gold, from digging in the earth, he describes the subjectivity, relativity, and insubstantiality of morality in terms reminiscent of Hamlet and Troilus:

> Gold?... Thus much of this will make
> Black white, foul fair, wrong right,
> Base noble, old young, coward valiant.
> Ha, you gods! Why this?...
> This yellow slave
> Will knit and break religions, bless th' accurs'd,
> ... place thieves,
> And give them title, knee, and approbation
> With senators on the bench.
>
> (IV.III.26–38)

But Timon's hatred of everyone is so extreme that when Alcibiades, the military commander, comes upon him in the forest and asks, "Is man so hateful to thee, That art thyself a man?," Timon replies, "I am Misanthropos, and hate mankind" – presumably including himself (IV.iv.52–4).

This conclusion is reinforced when Alcibiades says, "I am thy friend, and pity thee, dear Timon," yet Timon refuses even this free and unsolicited offer of friendship, saying, "I had rather be alone" (IV.iii.98–100). He is so consumed with hatred of the Athenians and by his desire for revenge against them that he rejects even help that would be in his "rational self-interest" to accept, were he still capable of caring for or loving even himself.

But there is something that Timon does want Alcibiades to do for him: destroy Athens and all its inhabitants. That is something Alcibiades is already motivated to do, since he has just been banished from the city (despite all that he had done in the not so distant past to save Athens from its enemies), because he had pleaded for mercy for one of his soldiers who had been sentenced to death for killing someone who had insulted him in a quarrel. In this respect, Alcibiades has a lot in common with Timon – intense anger and violent impulses in response to being rejected and insulted by the Athenians instead of receiving gratitude for all he had done for them. Knowing this, Timon gives some of the gold he has found to Alcibiades, telling him,

> With man's blood paint the ground, . . .
> Religious canons, civil laws are cruel;
> Then what should war be?
>
> (IV.iii.60–2)

And later in the same scene,

> by killing of villains
> Thou wast born to conquer my country.. . .
> Let not thy sword skip one.
> Pity not honor'd age for his white beard, . . .
> Spare not the babe, . . .
> mince it sans remorse.. . .
> Put armor on thine ears and on thine eyes,
> Whose proof nor yells of mothers, maids, nor babes,
> Nor sight of priests in holy vestments bleeding,
> Shall pierce a jot.
>
> (IV.iii.106–27)

In short, do not let your slaughter of everyone – man, woman, and child – be inhibited by feelings either of pity or guilt and remorse. (Today, of course, this would be called genocide, war crimes, and crimes against humanity.)

The one person Timon exempts from his wish for universal extermination of the whole human race is his loyal steward Flavius, whom he decides is the only honest person he knows. To Flavius he gives enough gold for him to be financially independent, yet with this advice:

> Hate all, curse all, show charity to none,
> But let the famish'd flesh slide from the bone
> Ere thou relieve the beggar. Give to dogs
> What thou deniest to men. Let prisons swallow 'em,
> Debts wither 'em to nothing.. . .
> And so farewell and thrive.
>
> (IV.iii.527–33)

Following this, Athenian senators visit Timon to apologize for their failure to help him out of his financial catastrophe, and they offer to make up for that by giving him "such heaps of love and wealth / As shall to thee blot out what wrongs were theirs" (V.i.153–4). They also offer him

"The captainship," which, if he accepts it, "thou shalt be met with thanks, / Allow'd with absolute power, and thy good name / Live with authority" (V.i.161–3). What they want in return is for Timon to shield them from Alcibiades' threatened assault on the city.

However, Timon rejects even this offer to return to him much more than he had lost, saying, "If Alcibiades kill my countrymen, . . . Timon cares not" (V.i.169–71). And, finally, he goes to his death, having composed another epitaph for himself: "Here lies a wretched corpse, of wretched soul bereft; . . . I, Timon, who, alive, all living men did hate" (V.iv.71–2).

What are we to make of this reversal from unrestrained philanthropy to equally uninhibited misanthropy? How can we understand what Shakespeare is showing us here? And what can we learn from it?

In the play, many characters describe Timon as having gone mad or lost his mind (his "wit"). Ironically, Timon himself, before he experienced his downfall and his character reversal, had criticized Apemantus for being so angry and misanthropic, quoting the Latin saying, "*Ira furor brevis est*" – anger is a brief madness – only to outdo Apemantus by far on that score by the end of the play.

Many critics have felt puzzled by Timon's behavior and have criticized Shakespeare in much the same way that Apemantus criticized Timon, namely, that "The middle of humanity thou never knewest, but the extremity, of both ends" (IV.iii.300–1). Apemantus meant that Timon had gone from extreme affluence to extreme poverty. But we could also say that he went from extreme philanthropy to extreme misanthropy. It seems to be much easier to understand and recognize people who are in the middle in terms of their personalities, moral values, and behavior than it is to understand those who are at the extremes. However, in the era in which we are currently living and have been living now for some time, it would seem essential to learn how to understand the extremes that we witness in Timon, not only among individuals, including those who are the most violent people in our society or others, but also among those who are members of extreme and extremely violent political groups – on a world-wide basis.

I (James Gilligan) have devoted my career to studying the most violent individuals our society produces, as well as the most violent political movements that have erupted in our nation and others. With the former, I found that the most violent among the men I saw in both American and foreign prisons and prison psychiatric hospitals would tell me that their goal in life (and death) was to go to their own death in a hail of gunfire, but only after killing as many other people as possible. Many of them behaved in that way within the prisons, going "berserk" and often provoking violent retaliation and self-defense from prison officers or other prisoners, at the risk of their own lives. And in the community, up to a thousand men every year in the United States, from teenagers to the middle-aged (almost never women) behave in precisely this way, murdering as many people as they can until they are either killed by the police or commit suicide with their last bullet. Some (the school shooters) do this in grade schools, high schools, or universities, others in a range of public places where crowds congregate. This phenomenon, when it includes being killed by the police, is so common that the police have a name for it: "suicide by cop." I have spoken with officers who felt traumatized themselves by feeling forced to kill someone because that was the only way they could get him to stop killing other people. (I need hardly add that this is not to be confused with police killings of unarmed or nonviolent people.)

When I have spoken with individuals who have expressed this fantasy in words but have not (yet) acted it out, the underlying emotion was the feeling that they had been overwhelmingly and irreparably humiliated, rejected, taunted, shamed, or betrayed, regarded as worthless, unlovable, or "treated like dirt." In other words, they felt much like Timon. One difference between Timon and most of these individuals, however, was that it was rare for them ever to have had a period of extreme affluence. Another was that, unlike Timon, they had committed the murders themselves, rather than, as Timon did, commissioning others to do the killing for them. Timon's way is the strategy that most powerful or affluent people employ when they have a similar goal and act it out on a political scale: they do not actually do the killing themselves.

We call this scale of violence, whether individual or national, "apocalyptic" because it amounts to acting out the fantasy of bringing about the end of the world, or at least the whole human world, including the perpetrator(s). No one has yet been able to cause destruction on a truly global scale, although now that we are in the era of thermonuclear weapons, whose proliferation we have shown ourselves incapable of preventing (so far), it may become increasingly possible for one or more, among the many national rulers of questionable sanity, to bring about destruction on a scale that is not limited to being genocidal but would actually be "humanicidal" (i.e., to kill all humanity, not just the members of one group) – as Timon expressed an interest in doing. Given this technological possibility, it is worth noticing that since the early twentieth century (beginning in the United States, but now throughout the world, in all of the major world religions), new religious ideologies called "apocalyptic fundamentalism" have been invented, and have endorsed terrorism as a political strategy. Terrorism can be considered one variety of genocide in the sense that, as in Timon's fantasies, it is a form of violence aimed at everyone in the population without exception: adults and children. The so-called suicide bombers, whose mass murders now occur virtually every day somewhere in the world, are an example of people who are so desperately eager to kill as many people as possible that they are willing to kill themselves as well in order to do so. Fundamentalist religions, even in the United States, indicate they would welcome the end of the world if and whenever that becomes possible. Indeed, the best-selling set of novels in American publishing history are devoted to precisely this fantasy (or goal), namely, that the world will come to an end in the near future, the fundamentalists will be elevated to heaven, and the nonbelievers will be "left behind."[1] Religious groups with at least a "family resemblance" to the American Christian fundamentalists are among the most powerful supporters of political extremism in Islamic, Jewish, Hindu, and Buddhist countries as well. In short, Timon of Athens is alive and well today, all around us – alive, but just as determined to die, though not before being as dedicated to bringing about the end of the world as Timon was.

Perhaps the closest analogy to Timon in the modern world was Adolf Hitler, who began by wanting to destroy all the members of whole national, ethnic, and religious groups, especially Jews – every man, woman, and child of them – and then, when he realized he had lost the war, ordered some of his successors, including Albert Speer, to destroy the German people and the German nation as well, because he felt they had failed and betrayed him by not winning the war for him.[2] Even though he had built his version of Nietzsche's "master morality" into his political movement, his countrymen had failed to be the "master race" that he envisioned them as. In *Timon of Athens*, Shakespeare once again can be seen as providing us with an "early warning signal" that was prophetic of

---

[1] *Left Behind* is a multimedia franchise that started with a series of sixteen best-selling religious novels by Tim LaHaye and Jerry B. Jenkins, published by Tyndale House Publishers, that dealt with Christian dispensationalist "End Times": the pretribulation, premillennial, Christian eschatological interpretation of the coming biblical apocalypse, published 1995–2007. This agenda is also promoted in *Left Behind: The Movie* (2000), and many other iterations.

[2] Shirer (1960), p. 1103: "Germany was to be made one vast wasteland. Nothing was to be left with which the German people might somehow survive their defeat."

developments that were only nascent at his time, but have ripened into the genocide and terrorism of the past century.

In what way was Timon's moral nihilism different – if it was – from that of Hamlet or Troilus? The main difference is that their moral nihilism stemmed from the loss of credibility of the traditional sources of moral (and hence also legal and political) authority, which in turn stemmed from the scientific revolution that altered people's minds by replacing faith with doubt as the path to knowledge. Whereas with Timon, it is not so much that he rejected or repudiated shame ethics or guilt ethics because of changes in the *Zeitgeist* that cost them their credibility. Instead, Timon believed in those ethics but discovered that they didn't work in practice. He had lived in a way that he could have felt satisfied the moral demands of both guilt ethics and shame ethics. With respect to the former, he was altruistic, and giving to others even at the expense of sacrificing much of his wealth. And he also satisfied the demands of shame ethics, because by virtue of having so much money he had proved how successful he was, and because he was giving so much of it to his guests, they flattered, honored, praised, and respected him. However, after he learned that he had bankrupted himself, he was humiliated by the discovery that his former guests did not honor him at all but treated him as they would treat any other beggar – or possibly even worse.

It is true that Timon ultimately proved to have been much more sensitive to the influence of shame ethics, not guilt ethics, all along, even though his generosity might have been mistaken for adherence to a guilt ethic. When Jesus told the rich man what he must do to be saved (and we are taking Jesus' moral code as the most extreme example of a guilt ethic), he did not say, "Give luxurious dinner parties for all of your rich friends." He said, "Give all thou hast to the poor, go and live with them and share your wealth with them" (Luke 14:12–14, 18:22; Matt. 19:22). And even Timon's servant Fulvia, who judged (or misjudged) Timon's generosity to have constituted moral goodness, recognized that no one in his world, including especially Timon himself, was following another of the ethical prescriptions of guilt ethics: love and forgive your enemies. On the contrary, he wanted to kill them all.

Timon's lavish gifts and entertainments bear some resemblance to the "potlatch" ceremonies of the Kwakiutl Indians, as described by Franz Boas and Ruth Benedict,[3] in which chieftains would compete with each other to show which of them was the wealthiest by giving or throwing away more

---

[3] Boas (1966); Benedict (1958).

and more valuable objects. By this means, the wealthiest one humiliated all the others and proved his superiority to them. And Thorstein Veblen[4] documented similar behavior on the part of wealthy Americans during the "Gilded Age" of the late nineteenth century, who would publicly prove how high their socioeconomic status was by means of what he called "conspicuous consumption" and "conspicuous waste" – again, much like Timon. If his behavior shamed his guests into feeling inferior because of his exhibiting to them how much wealthier he was than they were, that would at least explain two things: why they unanimously refused to help him out when he revealed he had bankrupted himself, and why he reacted to their ingratitude by swearing to get revenge on those whom he now felt were enemies rather than friends, rather than loving and forgiving his enemies (as he would have done if his generosity had been motivated from the beginning by a guilt ethic, rather than a shame ethic).

The fact that Timon was consumed with hate and the desire for revenge because of the humiliations his false friends had subjected him to is perhaps the clearest evidence that his only moral code was a shame ethic. But the failure of his shame ethic, whose precepts he followed most extremely, to guarantee him the respect, admiration, and gratitude from others that he had assumed it would led him to abandon even the major commandments of shame ethics, namely: look out for yourself first of all, be an opportunist, and whenever you have an opportunity to recoup your losses and restore your honor, take it! Timon, however, was so monopolized by hate of (almost) everyone and by his mission of revenge against the whole world that he forgot to make an exception and failed to love himself, at least. It is perhaps not so much that he rejected shame ethics as that he perished in the fires of revenge that it commanded him to set. Or to put it another way, he demonstrated, in his behavior, one of the reasons why shame ethics simply do not work, as the sole guide to one's behavior. If shame ethics commands one to love oneself and hate one's enemies, the latter of these two commandments so far outweighed the first that he drowned in his own hate. When shame and humiliation cut deep enough, there is sometimes no way back to enough pride and honor to make life worth living, to the person so affected, so the only way to anesthetize his emotional pain is by means of killing himself as well as everyone else in an apocalyptic *Götterdämmerung* (à la Hitler).

Thus it is not so much that Timon was unable to continue to believe in either of the two forms of morality because of their cognitive/

---

[4] Veblen (1953).

epistemological inadequacy, as Hamlet and Troilus did, as that he felt his moral codes had failed him in practical terms. For he had acted according to precepts of shame ethics and they had failed to deliver for him what he thought they had promised, namely, prestige, status, gratitude, admiration, love, honors, and so on. So his disappointment with shame ethics was not so much *cognitive* in nature – that it was not credible – as that it had failed in *practice*.

Shame ethics commands: *get revenge* when you have been humiliated. But when there is no limit to the amount of revenge you want to get, you can consume yourself in the fire with which you want to burn down the whole world. It is only in that sense – namely, his continued adherence to that commandment of shame ethics – that we speak of his violence as apocalyptic rather than being simply the product of moral agnosticism. That latter mental state, as exemplified by Hamlet and Troilus, causes paralysis and confusion more than activity (although that, in turn, can cause death, for the self and others). In Timon, moral nihilism would have inhibited him from formulating and pursuing in his behavior any moral goal, whether revenge or self-punishment. Whereas he is very actively following one of the main precepts of shame ethics: "Get revenge when you have been disrespected and dishonored!"

But Timon felt so deeply and irreparably humiliated that he simply gave up on the possibility of restoring his sense of pride and honor even by means of revenge. He knew he could hate and express and act out his hate; and he felt so irrevocably humiliated that he felt it would be impossible to achieve a resurrection of the self that they had mortified, so the only option he felt was open to him was to destroy the whole human species. The hatred stimulated by shame overwhelmed any path back to self-love; his emotions were entirely monopolized by his hate toward others, which was so extreme that he was willing to sacrifice his own interests and his own life in order to satisfy his wish to get revenge – much like the genocidal mass murderers, terrorist suicide-bombers, and other extreme political leaders of today.

CHAPTER 8

Transcending Morality, Preventing Violence
Measure for Measure, The Tempest, The Winter's Tale, *and* The Merchant of Venice

With its very title, Shakespeare tells us that in *Measure for Measure*, he will show the practice of men judging men, both morally and legally. For his title alludes to one of the most profound and radical, indeed revolutionary passages in Jesus' Sermon on the Mount: "Judge not that ye be not judged, for with what measure ye judge, ye shall be judged; and with what measure ye mete, it shall be measured to you again" (Matt. 7:1–2). This counsel to stop judging each other can be understood as a call to abandon moral value judgments altogether, and to recognize that only God knows how guilty and sinful, or virtuous and saintly, people are, and what punishments or rewards they deserve. As the Bible tells us, "Vengeance is mine, saith the Lord," meaning that no human knows, or can know, who is evil enough to deserve punishment, or revenge – with the added implication that we have all fallen short of the demands of morality to one degree or another, so that we all stand in need of forgiveness. Judging, condemning, or punishing others for their sinfulness, and thus taking revenge on them, can be hypocritical only in the sense of implying that the other person is guilty, whereas oneself is not. Since no men are good, only God has the "right" to punish anyone (Matt. 19:17).

But if this is the case, then are we not faced with moral nihilism and legal anomie? Certainly, one of the most eminent Shakespeare scholars, Harold Bloom, thought so. As he put it, "*Measure for Measure* surpasses the four High Tragedies [*Lear, Hamlet, Macbeth*, and *Othello*] as the masterpiece of nihilism," surpassing even those "forerunners of nineteenth-century European nihilism of Nietzsche's prophecies and Dostoevsky's obsessives.... [T]here are no values available in Vincentio's Vienna, since every stated or implied vision of morality, civil or religious, is either hypocritical or irrelevant."[1]

---

[1] Bloom (1998), p. 363.

Bloom is certainly correct if we focus on the obvious corruption of the whole concept of justice and morality by Angelo, the hypocrisy with which he threatens to use the power of the state to commit judicial murder and then uses that threat to pressure the ostensibly virtuous Isabella into submitting to rape by means of extortion, which is followed by her placing a higher value on her "honor" than on her brother's life (as if that made her into a better Christian), and on and on. Nevertheless, focusing on this aspect of the play, many of whose characters do display the most egregious hypocrisy, would miss what we see as the main point, and the more profound one, of *Measure for Measure*, namely, that what Bloom calls its absence of morality is actually its transcendence of morality. What Shakespeare is doing here is what Jesus described as his purpose when he said, "Think not that I am come to destroy the [moral] Law, or the prophets: I am not come to destroy, but to fulfill" (Matt. 5.17).

The achievement of that fulfillment is what *Measure for Measure*, along with the other plays we discuss in this chapter, dramatizes. We begin by noting that in each of these four plays Shakespeare shows us the replacement of retributive justice (punishment, or revenge, measured out in proportion to the measurement that the judge, or the law, makes of the amount of injustice the offender has inflicted on his victim and the community) with what has recently come to be called restorative justice – though we would prefer to call it the transcendence of the very concept of justice. By that we mean the concept of healing, education, reconciliation (between offenders and the individuals and communities whose peace and safety and trust they have violated); and the transformation of people who have been harming others and themselves into people who will help and heal instead. This makes it possible for their freedom to be restored without endangering anyone, as well as restoring to the community the potential these men (or women) have for making constructive contributions to the lives of others.

Measure for Measure begins with Vincentio, the Duke of Venice, pretending that he is going to leave Venice for an undetermined length of time, even though he will actually stay disguised as a friar in order to observe what happens during his "absence." Before he leaves, he appoints his deputy, Angelo, a man known for his exceptionally strict morality, to take his place during his absence. The excuse he gives for doing this (which is not his real reason) is that although Venice already has "strict statutes and most biting laws," he (the Duke) has failed to enforce them strictly. And, he says, in line with the popular theory that the fear of violent

punishment is the only sure means of preventing violent crime, he accuses
himself of having been like

> fond fathers,
> Having bound up the threat'ning twigs of birch,
> Only to stick it in their children's sight
> For terror, not to use, in time the rod
> [Becomes] more mocked than feared; so our decrees,
> Dead to infliction, to themselves are dead,
> And liberty plucks justice by the nose;
> The baby beats the nurse, and quite athwart
> Goes all decorum.
>
> (I.iii.23–31)

Parroting the conventional wisdom, he goes on to say, "When evil deeds
have their permissive pass, / And not the punishment" (38–9), people will
violate the laws of both morality and the legal system. Indeed, he goes so far as
to say that "'twas my fault to give the people scope," and he blames his own
permissiveness and nonpunitiveness for what he describes as an increase in
violations of the law (none of which is described in detail, or quantitatively – as
is true of many of the often imaginary "crime waves" in the world of today).

However, when describing what he is actually doing in pretending to
leave Vienna and appointing Angelo as his stand-in, Vincentio tells Friar
Thomas what in fact he is up to:

> More reasons for this action
> At our more leisure shall I render you;
> Only, this one: Lord Angelo is precise;
>   . . . scarce confesses
> That his blood flows; or that his appetite
> Is more to bread than stone: *hence we shall see*
> *If power change purpose: what our seemers be.*
>
> (I.iii.53–4, emphasis added)

Shakespeare quickly shows us the answer to these questions (does power
change purpose, and are Angelo and others what they seem to be?). For the
first thing the ostensibly moral Angelo does is to condemn Claudio to
death for committing the "crime" of having impregnated a women he loves
and wants to marry but whom he has not yet wed. In response to Angelo's
plan to commit judicial murder, Isabella, Claudio's sister, gives one of the
most powerful and moving speeches in any of Shakespeare's plays:

> man, proud man,
> Dress'd in a little brief authority,

Most ignorant of what he's most assur'd
   [namely, of what justice is and what it requires],
(His glassy essence), like an angry ape
Plays such fantastic tricks before high heaven
As makes the angels weep.

                (II.ii.117–22)

Yet following Isabella's moral criticism, Angelo reveals to her that behind his moralism, which has led him to condemn her brother to death for having sex outside marriage, he wants to have sex with her – also outside marriage – but in this case even outside any desire for it on her part. Given the patriarchal morality he is invoking, it hardly seems surprising that Angelo finds Isabella especially tempting to have sex with precisely because of her unusually extreme commitment to her virginity. For that could be counted on to spare him from the risk of suffering the shame and dishonor of loving a woman who has slept with, or potentially could sleep with, other men. To put it concisely, in a shame culture, a woman's honor depends more on her chastity than on anything else; and a man's honor, on the chastity and sexual fidelity of the woman he is involved with, as much as on anything else. It then follows that Isabella, this would-be nun who has committed herself to strict sexual continence, is much more appealing to Angelo's male vanity than any more sexually liberal young woman could be or, in his experience, ever has been.

However, Isabella's own moral valuations are equally complicated: understandable, but also destructive and hypocritical. When Angelo gives her the choice of sleeping with him or having her brother murdered, she has no hesitation, indeed no ambivalence, in preferring that her brother be murdered than that she sacrifice her virginity to save his life. In defense of her feelings, it cannot be denied that Angelo is resorting to blatant extortion, and that if she were to submit to his demand for what to her is unwanted sexual activity, she would in effect be submitting to what could be considered the equivalent of rape – one of the ultimate humiliations that a man can subject a woman to.

So it is part of the moral incoherence of patriarchy that a man would expect that a woman who is devoting her life to Christianity and its guilt ethic not only would but also *should* expose herself to shame and dishonor if that is the only way to save her brother's life. After all, Jesus subjected himself to "shame and spitting" in order to save the lives of all of us.

But the patriarchal moral code of shame cultures also demands that a woman should make the opposite moral valuation and regard her renunciation of extramarital sex as her *most* morally important characteristic, for the loss of her chastity would condemn her to eternal and irretrievable shame and dishonor (hence Lucretia's suicide after being raped by Tarquin, as her response to even an involuntary sexual act).

It is not lightly that we question Isabella's response to the insoluble moral dilemma that Angelo has imposed on her – for whatever choice she makes is moral in terms of one of the two codes of morality, but equally, limitlessly and unforgivably immoral, in terms of the other.

What we are more interested in here is Isabella's own moral reflections on her dilemma. And it is a dilemma because she has more than one choice – even more than one morally defensible one. When Claudio points out that "of the deadly seven" sins, sexual offenses are "the least" (III.i.110), he is overlooking the fact that "lust," the sin he is referring to, exists (for the woman) only if she herself has *desired* the sexual act. However, what Isabella is confronted with is a demand for sex that she herself does *not* desire, which exposes her to shame, not sin. So that when Claudio reminds her that "Death is a fearful thing," her reply is "And shamed life a hateful" (III.i.115–16) – as though protecting herself from shame is more important than protecting him from death.

To be clear, for Isabella, submitting to Angelo's extortion would be more a violation of a shame ethic, a disgrace or dishonor, than a sin (a violation of a guilt ethic). Claudio is right when he observes,

> What sin you do to save a brother's life,
> Nature dispenses with the deed so far,
> That it becomes a virtue.
>
> (III.i.133–5)

What Isabella was presenting as saintliness is as phony as Angelo's even more pretentious hypocrisy. Ironically, Angelo and Isabella collude with each other to bring about Claudio's murder, and they both do so while portraying themselves as models of moral righteousness. Although it is Angelo, not Isabella, who initiates the move to murder Claudio, Isabella in effect seconds the motion.

Isabella's insistence that her chastity is more important than her brother's life recalls Parolles' cynical comment, in *All's Well That Ends Well*, that "virginity is peevish, proud, idle, made of self-love, which is the most inhibited sin in the canon" (I.i.144–5). That is, the desire to preserve one's virginity is motivated more by the desire to protect one's self-love or pride, and to avoid their opposites, shame and dishonor, than by the desire to avoid sin or guilt. And the deadliest of the seven deadly sins is pride, whereas the least sinful is lust. However, we must acknowledge that Parolles' remark is the argument that patriarchal men make when they are trying to persuade a woman to have sex with them outside marriage, as

opposed to the horror and condemnation they have when women do have
sex outside marriage.

It is difficult to see Isabella as a model of Christian virtue when she
replies to Claudio's plea that she sacrifice her virginity to save his life, for
then she becomes almost vicious in her anger at him for valuing his own
life more highly than her virginity:

> O you beast!
> O faithless coward! O dishonest wretch!
> Wilt thou be made a man out of my vice?
> Is't not a kind of incest, to take life
> From thine own sister's shame?. . .
> Die, perish!. . .
> I'll pray a thousand prayers for thy death,
> No word to save thee.. . .
> Thy sin's not accidental [a chance happening], but a trade [established practice].
>   Mercy to thee would prove itself a bawd,
> 'Tis best that thou diest quickly.
>
>   (III.i.135–50)

With these words, Isabella proves herself fully as capable as Angelo is of
being motivated by moral reasons to murder Claudio and his beloved – for
the crime of loving and having sex, conceiving a child, and being eager to
marry! Thus does morality stimulate murder, not only of existing life and
love, but even of future life! Not for nothing does the Duke comment that
"there is so great a fever on goodness [i.e., goodness – morality – is causing
so much death], that the dissolution of it must cure it" (i.e., only the
dissolution of morality will end the violent deaths that are being caused by
morality) (III.ii.222–3). But the Duke's comment is not an expression of
moral nihilism; it is a description of the need to transcend morality, and its
destructiveness, by replacing it with love.

And in fact the Duke, when he finally abandons his disguise, does dissolve
morality – in a bath of love and forgiveness, and also with a withering
demonstration of the destructiveness and irrationality of morality. First, he
orders Isabella to forget justice and forgive Angelo, despite Angelo's crimes
of attempted murder and attempted rape, along with his betrayal and
abandonment of Mariana, to whom he was legally betrothed. The Duke
orders her to do this for Mariana's sake as well as for Angelo's, since Mariana
loves Angelo and wants him to live – which is clearly more important in
promoting love and life than justice for Angelo himself would be. But the
Duke also shows the opposite, the death and destruction that justice, were it
honored, would lead to. Speaking of Angelo, he tells Isabella,

> but as he adjudg'd your brother –
> Being criminal, in double violation
> Of sacred chastity and of promise-breach,
> Thereon dependent for your brother's life –
> The very mercy of the law cries out
> Most audible, even from his proper tongue,
> "An Angelo for Claudio, death for death!"
> Haste still pays haste, and leisure answers leisure;
> Like doth quit like, and *Measure* still *for Measure.*
> Then Angelo, . . .
> We do condemn thee to the very block
> Where Claudio stoop'd to death.
>
> (V.i.403–15)

Of course, Vincentio only pretends that Claudio has been killed and that Angelo will be killed, partly as a way of impressing on all concerned how irreversible death is, how incomparably more important it is than all of our quotidian and recoverable losses, and how close all the participants in this drama had been to imposing such a loss on persons whom some of them loved, and with all of whom they shared a common humanity. Both Mariana and Isabella, despite how hurtfully Angelo had treated both of them, plead that he be forgiven and allowed to live. Angelo himself recovers (or achieves) a capacity for guilt and remorse and asserts that he deserves death, not mercy.

To all of this the Duke replies with the same response: he forgives the guilty, and bids them to love and be reconciled with one another, and to harm no one else in the future. To better guarantee the last point, he pardons the alcoholic murderer Barnardine but hands him over to the Friar for ongoing advisement. He permits (or orders) Angelo to marry Mariana, saying, "Love your wife; her worth worth yours" (V.i.497). And "Joy to you, Mariana! Love her, Angelo!" (V.i.526).

Even Lucio, "whose slanders I forgive, and therewithal remit thy other forfeits," is ordered to marry the woman he had impregnated – his forced marriage being punishment enough. To Isabella, he says, "Give me your hand, and say you will be mine" (V.i.492), and "if you'll a willing ear incline, / What's mine is yours, and what is yours is mine" (V.i.536–7). By that latter equivocation, "if," the Duke may be seen as leaving the door open for her refusal, if she does not want to accede to his wish to marry her – without threatening her with any punishment if she chooses not to.

In his speech to Claudio, Duke Vincentio summarizes what he has done: "She, Claudio, that [woman] you wronged [by impregnating her before marrying her], look you restore." And that word, "restore," is the final clue telling us what the Duke is accomplishing here. For it is the word that is still being used to describe the difference between "retributive justice" and "restorative justice." As the words imply, the purpose of retributive justice is retribution, or in other words, revenge and violence: the deliberate infliction of as much pain on the offender as they have inflicted on their victim – measure for measure, an eye for an eye, a death for a death. Punishment is violence, for the purpose of revenge, administered by the state's criminal justice system, rather than by the victim or the victim's family.

The word "justice" becomes a euphemism for revenge when it is used to justify retribution. The Greek and Latin roots of the word "punishment" reveal this much about our cultural unconscious: *poine* and *poena* are the sources of the words pain, penal system, penalty, punitive, and punishment. And in Greek and Latin, respectively, they mean revenge. Indeed, Poine was the name of the Greek goddess of revenge. So punishment is the gratuitous and unnecessary infliction of pain for the sake of achieving revenge, which is still the standard model of most criminal justice systems in the world, though much more so in the United States, which has, by many criteria, the most punitive criminal justice system in the world.[2]

The purpose of restorative justice, in contrast to retributive, is not punishment, violence, retribution, or revenge. Its means and its end are reform of the offender, reconciliation between the offender and their community (including their victims), and restoration, to the victim and the community of what the offender had taken from them, most importantly, peace of mind – the ability to trust one's fellow citizens not to harm, injure, or betray them. In fact, Shakespeare does not call what he is showing us here "justice" at all. He only uses the word "restore" to refer to what he is getting at. So we could also say that restorative justice would more accurately be called the transcendence of justice, and the abandonment of the quest for justice (meaning by "justice" the illusion that we are capable of measuring how much injustice a person has committed and how much punishment would equal that measurement), and the replacement of the quest of justice with the goal of preventing violence and injury, death, and disability by everyone involved: individuals and the state.

This describes what Shakespeare has his protagonists accomplish, not only in *Measure for Measure*, but to one degree or another in *The Tempest*, *The Winter's Tale*, and even *The Merchant of Venice*. In each of these plays,

---

[2] Ferguson (2014).

Shakespeare gives us a model for the prevention of violence – not only the violence of individual offenders (called "criminals") but also the violence inflicted by the state, which is potentially more dangerous, since the state has so much more power than all the individual offenders put together. In *Measure for Measure*, for example, Angelo is prevented from using the power and authority of the state to commit legalized murder, but he himself is not murdered by the state, or even imprisoned, when his own culpability is discovered. Instead, he is reconciled with his intended victims, including Isabella and Mariana, both of whom forgive him and plead that he not be punished.

Shakespeare, as we have claimed, is the first psychologist of post-medieval Europe ("first" both chronologically and qualitatively, i.e., the one with the greatest depth of insight into human psychology). His play *Measure for Measure* can be seen as one elaborate and extended social-psychological experiment designed to test several closely related hypotheses, including (but not limited to) the following:

1. To "see / If power change purpose" (I.iii.53–4) or, in other words, do people abandon and violate the moral principles they claim and appear to believe in, after they are given the power to inflict punishment, or retributive justice, on other people? (For example, Angelo.)
2. Are the most moral people – the ones who impose the strictest moral commandments on themselves and others – the least violent? Or in other words, does morality prevent violence? (For example, Angelo and Isabella.)
3. Does punishment – the infliction of pain and even death – prevent violence? Or in other words, do people become less violent the more strictly they or others are punished, even for minor violations of the law? The belief that they will is part of the now largely discredited "broken windows" and "zero tolerance" theories of crime prevention. These theories include the belief that inflicting severe punishments for minor crimes ("loitering," failing to pay a subway fare, and so on, in the contemporary United States, or engaging in premarital sex, in Shakespeare's time), and even defining and punishing these nonviolent behaviors as crimes at all, will prevent violence. Rather than achieving that goal, the policies stimulated by these theories, when subjected to rigorous analysis, have shown no replicable, demonstrable effect except to increase police harassment of blacks and the poor, and to have stimulated more violence, on the part of the police and the people targeted by them.

4. And conversely, do people become more violent the less severely they are punished?
5. Is it possible that rejecting the practice of punishing people altogether might result in less violence overall, both by individuals and by the criminal "justice" system? Or in other words, are "fond fathers" (I.i.23) actually likely to have less violent children?

The events of the play can be seen as Shakespeare's way of showing us the answers to all of those questions. For what he has shown us here is exactly what all of our current empirical research has confirmed, namely, that far from preventing violence, and thus making the community safer, punishment is the most powerful cause of violence that we have yet discovered.[3] The more severely children are punished, the more violent they become, both as children and after they become adults. The more severely adults are punished, as by the death penalty, the higher the murder rates are – whether comparing the differences between the US states that inflict death penalties and those that do not, or comparing different nations. The United States is the only Western democracy that still has the death penalty, and its murder rates are five to ten times higher than the average of those in the countries of Western Europe and the other English-speaking democracies, which do not commit this form of judicial murder.

The United States has the highest imprisonment rate in the world – higher than in countries that we call "police states," and ten times higher than the countries of Western Europe – and yet our murder rates are by far the highest among all of the economically developed nations of the world (e.g., ten times higher than England's). The United States is the only one among the developed nations that still imposes prolonged, uninterrupted solitary confinement (up to thirty years, in some cases) on its prisoners, a form of punishment that is considered "torture" by the United Nations and the European Court of Justice.

The most violent of the individual violent criminals in the United States are themselves the victims of the most extreme violent child abuse: they are the survivors of their own attempted murders, usually by their own parents or by witnesses and survivors of the actual murders of their closest family members – a mother, father, sibling, or other relative. If punishment would prevent violence, these men would never have become violent in

---

[3] Gilligan (2000); Gilligan (2019); Gilligan (2021).

the first place, because they have already been punished as severely as it is possible to punish someone without actually killing them.

Duke Vincentio's experiment shows the answers to his questioning of the conventional wisdom that stricter enforcement of draconian punishments will result in less violence. His experiment confirms that giving the state (in the person of Angelo) the power to commit judicial murder and other punishments leads neither to violence prevention nor to any defensible definition of justice; instead, it leads to more violence, which is rationalized as justice but is actually just hypocrisy. By the end of the play, the Duke does not even claim to be pursuing justice and does not bother to ask what would constitute "justice." He is seeking to reconcile offenders and victims with each other and to restore to victims and the community, by his continued renunciation of violence, the trust in other people that the offender has taken from them.

Thus Duke Vincentio has not permitted violence by his permissiveness. He has actually stopped whatever violence was currently in progress (murder and rape), so no one is being allowed to continue to commit either of those forms of violence. In response to violence, he is not provoking further violence but is offering everyone involved a peaceful and constructive alternative.

In *The Tempest*, Prospero has been deposed from his position as Duke of Milan by his younger brother Antonio and the King of Naples. Exiled to an island, he hones his skills in sorcery. Twelve years later, when a storm tosses a ship carrying his brother and the king and his company onto the island, Prospero's helper, the spirit Ariel, entices the king's son Ferdinand to Prospero's cave, where he meets Prospero's daughter Miranda, and they fall in love with each other. After testing Ferdinand's sincerity, Prospero give him his assent to marry Miranda. Ariel then brings Antonio and the king to Prospero. They beg his forgiveness, which he grants in return for their agreement to restore his dukedom to him (a rather literal example of restorative justice). The play ends with Prospero planning to return to Naples with his former enemies to celebrate the marriage of the young couple. In the course of the play, Prospero has foiled several plots. Antonio and the king's brother Sebastian had plotted to murder the king; and Stephano, Trinculo, and Caliban, to seize the island for themselves. Prospero does this without killing any of them, and he neither kills nor punishes Antonio or the king. In fact, he reconciles with them and achieves the reconciliation of Sebastian and Antonio with the king. All this is the stuff of pure fantasy and imagination, of course, as is *Measure for Measure*. But what it is the imagining of is a world of restorative justice or, more exactly, as we said earlier, the placing of a higher value on love, forgiveness, reconciliation, the repair and restoration of relationships that had been shattered or violated, and the prevention of further violence than on the execution of retribution or revenge for past violence (in the name of justice and morality).

The Winter's Tale provides us with a further imaginative depiction of how violence is caused, how it can be forgiven, how previous enemies can be reconciled, and how future violence can be prevented. The play opens with the visit of Polixenes, king of Bohemia, to his childhood friend Leontes, the king of Sicilia. As someone obsessed with fear of being shamed by becoming a cuckold, Leontes accuses Polixenes of having seduced his wife and queen, Hermione. As a result, he orders his courtier, Camillo, to poison Polixenes (rather like Othello, except that he seeks the death not of his wife but of the man he suspects of being her lover). Camillo, however, who knows that Polixenes is innocent, informs Polixenes of Leontes' plan to kill him, and he flees with Polixenes to Bohemia. Believing that their flight confirms his suspicions, Leontes puts his wife in prison, where she gives birth to a daughter. He suspects that the daughter is the child of Polixenes and orders that she be abandoned.

Unknown to Leontes, however, Perdita, the lost daughter, is rescued by a shepherd in Bohemia, where she had been taken. When Mamilius, Leontes' son dies because of his grief over his mother's imprisonment and trial for adultery, Leontes is told that Hermione also died, from her grief over Mamilius' death. And at this point, Leontes finally begins to realize how much suffering and death his jealous and self-righteous mind has caused.

Sixteen years later, Perdita is discovered by the son of Polixenes, Florizel, who falls in love with her, and Camillo takes them all on a visit to Sicilia. There they discover proof that Perdita is the lost daughter of Leontes and Hermione. Anticipating the marriage of Perdita and Florizel, Leontes mourns the loss and absence of Hermione. He had thought she was dead though she had actually been secretly living in seclusion until her daughter could be restored to her.

As in *Measure for Measure* and *The Tempest*, there are no murders in *The Winter's Tale*. Although there are deaths (of Mamilius) and attempted murders (of Polixenes and Perdita), the play overcomes loss and past violence with love, forgiveness, reconciliation, and the restoration of all the remaining, previously violated relationships. No one is obsessed with questions of justice, punishment, or revenge, and there is no clear risk of any further violence.

The Merchant of Venice is a more complicated dramatization of what we are talking about here. We realize that many people would agree with Harold Bloom that "One would have to be blind, deaf and dumb not to recognize that Shakespeare's grand, equivocal comedy *The Merchant of Venice* is nevertheless a profoundly anti-Semitic work."[4] We can understand why many people would read it as just that. However, we read it not as an anti-Semitic play, but rather, as a play about anti-Semitism. Even Bloom comments that he does not believe that "Shakespeare was personally either anti-Semitic or philo-Semitic."[5] But it could be seen as a case study illustrating two points: how much less effective restorative justice is when it is compromised, by being combined with retribution and (financial) revenge, and how much less destructive retributive justice is when it is compromised, by being combined with forgiveness and the renunciation of (physical) revenge, that is, violence.

The Merchant of Venice could certainly be used to support anti-Semitism; but it could just as easily be used to condemn anti-Semitism, for it reveals in stunning detail the hypocrisy, cruelty, and destructiveness of this particular prejudice. But we do not see Shakespeare as playing the role of a moralist and either condoning or condemning anti-Semitism. Instead, he is showing how destructive and cruel anti-Semitism is, even when it limits itself to social and psychological humiliation and financial penalties and does not cross the boundary – as it has so often, historically – into physical violence.

Shakespeare does not himself make value judgments. He lets his characters speak for themselves and leaves it to his audience to draw their own conclusions. He holds up a mirror to the world and asks us to see what of ourselves and our world we see reflected in it. And much of what we see in this play, just as in the world, is appalling, and worth learning how to avoid. But Shakespeare also shows what could be, and sometimes is, even in the worst situations, beneficial and worth learning from – such as how to move the world in the direction, never to be fully attained, of love, forgiveness, and mutual respect. He also shows the costs to everyone when this is not achieved, or is achieved only partially.

In play after play, Shakespeare shows how deeply people are wounded when they feel shamed and humiliated, and how powerfully those emotions stimulate feelings of anger and wishes for revenge – and *The Merchant of Venice* is no exception. What this means is that the ultimate source of the violence in his plays is the person or group that does the shaming and humiliating, not the shamed person who is shamed into

---

[4] Bloom (1998), p. 171.   [5] Ibid., p. 175.

committing the acts of violence. In *Merchant* it is abundantly clear that Shylock has been systematically and repeatedly humiliated, as he says to Antonio, by "the shames that you have stain'd me with" (I.iii.139). Elsewhere, referring to Antonio, he says (correctly), "He hates our sacred nation" (I.iii.48). And speaking to Antonio, he reminds him that

> many a time and oft
> In the Rialto, you have rated [berated] me . . .
> You call me misbeliever, cut-throat dog,
> And spit upon my Jewish gabardine . . .
> You . . . did void your rheum [spittle] upon my beard
> And foot me as you spurn [kick] a stranger cur . . .
> you spit on me on Wednesday last,
> You spurn'd me such a day, another time
> You call'd me dog.
>
> 　　　　　　　　　　　　　　(I.iii.106–28)

Far from denying this or apologizing, Antonio says, "I am as like to call thee so again, / To spit on thee again, to spurn thee too," and calls himself "thine enemy" (I.iii.130–5).

Following this interchange, Shylock notes that Antonio "hath disgraced me, . . . laugh'd at my losses, mock'd at my gains, scorn'd my nation, . . . cool'd my friends, heated mine enemies: and what's his reason? I am a Jew" (III.i.54–8). He then mentions that if he chooses revenge for this, it is only because he is following the example of the Christians among whom he is living, who have no hesitation in seeking revenge if a Jew wrongs them: "The villainy you teach me, I will execute" (III.i.68–72).

And when he is in court, arguing for the right to claim his pound of flesh from Antony, and the judge reprimands him for not showing mercy, he reminds the court of the fact that his Christian neighbors, for all their talk of mercy, are not expected to free their slaves because "The slaves are ours." And the pound of flesh, as he says, is just as legally his, as a matter of law, as their slaves are the property of the Christians.

So how does Shakespeare solve this terrible conflict between Shylock the Jew and his Christian neighbors? During Shakespeare's lifetime, and in fact, ever since 1290, when Jews were expelled from England, there were very few Jews in the population, and most of them were probably converts to Christianity. One of those few was Queen Elizabeth's Jewish physician, Dr. Lopez, a Portuguese *converso* who was sentenced to be hanged and drawn and quartered, possibly because of a false accusation that he had been plotting to poison the queen. But of course Protestant and Catholic Christians had been killing each other profligately in England ever since

Henry VIII broke with the Catholic Church. So if Shakespeare simply wanted to show how easily religious differences could explode into extreme violence, he had plenty of examples from which to work.

The Merchant of Venice is often seen as an example of how viciously Jews were caricatured and slandered in Christian England, by being depicted as murderous anti-Christians. And this play is certainly vulnerable to that criticism. But as we read the play, it seems to us that Shakespeare is portraying the behavior and attitudes of the Christians who are persecuting Shylock in a way that would make it very hard to see them as anything other than hypocrites who, ironically, exemplify the truth in Bassiano's observation that

> In religion,
> What damned error but some sober brow
> Will bless it, and approve it with a text . . .
> There is no [vice] so simple but assumes
> Some mark of virtue on his outward parts.
> (III.ii.77–82)

Compared with the behavior of the so-called Christians in this play (and in Elizabeth's England), Shylock's behavior is no more violent than theirs. As Christians committed a judicially ordered murder of Dr. Lopez, Shylock is merely seeking a judicially ordered murder of Antonio. He shows complete respect for the rule of law, and at no point does he violate the limits of the law, even when he loses his case in court. But that does not mean that Shakespeare is defending or justifying Shylock's murderous intent. He is showing it, and showing what has caused it – namely, the systematic humiliation of Shylock by his anti-Semitic neighbors. It is their hypocrisy – rationalizing cruelty, greed, and revenge on grounds of a religion founded by a Jew who advocated treating everyone with love and forgiveness, *especially* those whom one sees as enemies – that is repeatedly shown in this play. So to focus only on Shylock's attempt to get revenge on someone who was repeatedly insulting him, while ignoring the financial revenge that the court inflicted on Shylock as well as the humiliations his neighbors inflicted on him, could be seen as itself a manifestation of anti-Semitism.

In sum, all the characters in this play, both Shylock and his pseudo-Christian antagonists, pursue retributive justice and revenge, but all of them also keep their retribution and revenge within legal and financial limits. Shylock seeks to have the court order Antonio's murder, but he commits no violence whatsoever on his own. And his antagonists commit no violence against him: he is not imprisoned, or tortured, or murdered. And in fact there are some elements of restorative justice in the court's final decision. For example, although Shylock's estate is reduced by half, his daughter will have her inheritance of that half restored to her (otherwise, she would have received nothing). Instead of being imprisoned (or worse), Shylock is restored to the community of law-abiding citizens of Venice. Antonio's peace of mind – his freedom from the fear of being murdered – is restored to him. And so on.

But what this play shows most clearly is how much less effective restorative justice is when it is so deeply compromised by or mixed together with a degree of retributive justice that is cruel, destructive, and unnecessary, and actually hampers and limits ongoing life rather than supporting and enhancing it. For example, because of the court's decisions, Shylock has lost both his livelihood and half of his capital – and for no constructive reason. One could read this is as another of Shakespeare's dramatizations of the destructiveness of retributive justice, with its goal of revenge, as opposed to restorative justice, with its goal of restoring to everyone involved what they had lost.

One reason we are so struck by Shakespeare's depiction of the replacement of retributive justice with restorative justice is that I (James Gilligan) spent almost ten years evaluating a violence-prevention experiment devoted to comparing the two. In the late 1990s the sheriff of the City and County of San Francisco, who administered their jails, together with his program director, asked me to design and evaluate a randomized, controlled experiment to compare the effect these two different approaches had on the frequency and severity of violent behavior committed by those who had been sentenced to jail for violent behavior in the community.[6]

The restorative justice project consisted of immersing an entire sixty-four-man cell block in an intensive program of structured activities for twelve hours per day, six days per week. Among the activities were two hours per day of group psychotherapy in small groups; the writing of a one-act play recreating an incident in their lives that had turned them toward a life of violence, followed by casting fellow inmates or volunteers from the community in performing and then discussing the play; spending two or three hours, once or twice weekly, with a series of victims of violence, or the survivors of murder victims, giving them a chance to impress on the inmates how much human suffering violence causes; plus

[6] Gilligan and Lee (2004); Gilligan and Lee (2005); Lee and Gilligan (2005); Schwartz (2009).

a variety of artistic and creative activities (art studios, writing poetry, etc.), together with academic educational activities.

The psychotherapy activity, which included a second-by-second reconstruction of what had been going on in the minds of each of them during the events leading up to their committing the violent act for which they had been incarcerated, revealed how uniformly these violent men assumed that the human world was divided into the superior and the inferior. In this hierarchical, patriarchal worldview, men are defined as superior, and women as inferior; and to be a "real" man, a man has to be superior not only to women but also to other men. This is a perfect recipe for the production of violence, for these men were terrified that they would lose their manhood – meaning their selves – if they let a woman challenge their domination, or let another man disrespect or insult them or treat them as inferior. The only means of preventing this that they knew of was to resort to violence.

Prior to these intense and detailed reviews of what was going on in their minds in the minutes leading up to their committing an act of violence, the men in the San Francisco jails experiment had not realized that they were making those assumptions. They just thought that this was the way the world is, that this was reality itself, simply the way the human world is constructed – which isn't questioned, just adapted to. Once they realized they had these assumptions, they saw how absurd and arbitrary they were, how destructive to themselves and others, and how much more sense other assumptions made. They spoke of themselves as having been "brainwashed" by our whole society from the time they were children. And they wanted to teach the new men coming into the jail what they had learned about themselves. Consequently, they were trained and encouraged to lead these therapy groups themselves, both in the jail and after they returned to the community – in churches, boys' clubs, after-school activities, twelve-step programs, and so on – just as alcoholics are often the best leaders of AA groups.

Before this Resolve to Stop the Violence Program (RSVP) was started, roughly 60 percent of the men in the cellblock had committed an act of violence serious enough to warrant a disciplinary hearing (beatings, stabbings, rapes, robberies, etc.), and that rate continued each year in a "control group" of otherwise identical violent offenders in a traditional retributive justice cellblock, oriented toward punishment rather than therapy, education, restoration to the community, and reconciliation between victims and violators (in this case, between these men and their families – for 50 percent of them were sent to the jail for crimes of domestic violence).

The results were astounding. The rate of in-house violence dropped to zero for a full year at a time; and the rate of violent reoffending, after these men had been in this program for as little as four months and were released from jail, was 83 percent lower than in those who were in the control group. The reduction in reincarceration was so huge that this program – even though it was more expensive, per inmate, than a traditional jail – saved the taxpayers four dollars for every dollar spent on it. More importantly, it made the community much safer. As a result, it received a major national prize for "innovations in American governance" from the Kennedy School of Government at Harvard. Naturally, it was opposed by right-wing politicians, who claimed that it amounted to being "soft on crime." As a result of this, the sheriff's department had to substantially reduce it.

Our point here is that our whole nation and other nations around the world have much to learn from Shakespeare's plays about the effectiveness of restorative justice in preventing those who have committed or intend to commit serious acts of violence from doing so in the future. More particularly, in *Measure for Measure*, *The Tempest*, *The Winter's Tale*, and *The Merchant of Venice*, Shakespeare dramatizes the need to transcend a morality that ironically stimulates violence in the name of justice, and to do so by fostering reconciliation and the restoring of relationships.

CHAPTER 9

The Form and Pressure of Shakespeare's Time and Ours

What *Shakespeare Shows Us about Shame, Guilt, Love, and Violence*

Hamlet was the pivotal play – not only in Shakespeare's body of plays but also in holding up a mirror to the "age and body" of an era that was indeed a pivotal time. And Shakespeare himself was the pivotal writer of his time: as the first psychologist in the post-medieval world, he stood astride the gap that had opened up between the medieval world of faith and superstition (the world of ghosts and witches), and the world of modern science (including the science of psychology).

Harry Levin, the late Shakespeare critic, observed: "Since plays can be vehicles for ideas, as [*Hamlet*] has so spectacularly been, we can illuminate it by our recourse to the history of ideas."[1] With that in mind, we quote Alfred North Whitehead's diagnosis of the scientific revolution that was in effect creating a cognitive earthquake by dividing the medieval from the modern mind at exactly the time at which Shakespeare was writing: "The Reformation, for all its importance, may be considered as a domestic affair of the European races.... It is quite otherwise with the rise of modern science.... Since a babe was born in a manger, it may be doubted whether so great a thing has happened with so little stir."[2] Or as the British historian Sir Herbert Butterfield put it,[3] the scientific revolution

> outshines everything since the rise of Christianity and reduces the Renaissance and Reformation to the rank of mere episodes, mere internal displacements within the system of medieval Christendom ... [It] looms so large as the real origin both of the modern world and of the modern mentality that our customary periodization of European history has become an anachronism and an encumbrance.

---

[1] Levin (1959).   [2] Whitehead (1948), pp. 1–2.   [3] Butterfield (1959), p. viii.

Thus Harry Levin entitled his study of the plays *Shakespeare and the Revolution of the Times*, for Shakespeare himself, who as we have observed was born in the same year as Galileo, referred many times to his age as "unquiet, . . . wild, . . . rotten, . . . heavy, . . . miserable, . . . dangerous, and troublous."[4]

But why was science so incompatible with the worldview of the Middle Ages? And why should it create so much anxiety and perturbation? When we speak of the medieval worldview, we are referring to the epistemological assumption on which medieval thinking was based, stated over and over again in a number of iterations by St. Augustine, at the very beginning of the transition from the Roman Empire to the Holy Roman Empire and medieval Christendom: *Credo ut intelligam*, or "I believe in order to understand." This meant, among other things, that if one wanted to understand how and when and why the world and human beings were created, or how we should behave, one had to have faith in the Revelation given by God to the prophets and Jesus, as written in the Bible and interpreted by the Church. In short, knowledge begins with an act of faith.

As late as the sixteenth century, as the French historian Lucien Febvre has documented, it was for all practical purposes impossible to doubt the basic principles of the faith that was propagated by the Church, for there was no other credible belief system.[5] Nor did the Protestant Reformation change this mindset: Luther placed faith at the center of his theology even more firmly than the Catholic Church had, claiming that faith alone – *fides solus* – was required for salvation, even more than virtuous behavior.

However, with the scientific revolution that started in the mid-sixteenth century with Copernicus' aptly named masterpiece *De Revolutionibus*, and also with the skepticism of Montaigne (Shakespeare was clearly aware of the ideas of both of them), the epistemological monopoly held by faith was replaced by its diametrical opposite: doubt. As Descartes, the man who has been called the first modern philosopher (or the first philosopher of modernity), put it in the first generation after Shakespeare's death, *De omnibus dubitandum est*: "Doubt everything" or "Everything is doubtable." This motto summarizes the epistemology of science, which is *take nothing on faith*: believe only in those hypotheses that have been confirmed (and not yet disconfirmed) by empirical data (testing and observation). And even then, believe them only provisionally and temporarily, until the

---

[4] Levin (1976).
[5] Febvre (1982): "the idea of constructing a metaphysical or moral system outside of religion had never occurred to any author before 1533" (p. 15).

hypotheses or the evidence are disconfirmed or changed by discrepant data, or replaced by theories with greater power to explain, predict, and control whatever phenomena are being studied.

What this meant for Western civilization was captured two centuries later by Nietzsche, who called it "the death of God" – thus describing what Copernicus began when he refuted biblical cosmology, and thus biblical inerrancy, and thus the Church's infallibility. Copernicus, himself a priest, was so aware of how fundamental and heretical an attack on the Church and the Christian religion (of that time) his theory of the solar system would be taken to be that he not only kept it from being published until after his death but also attempted to mitigate its offensiveness to the Church by describing it as merely a method of simplifying the astronomical calculations naval navigators needed to make. He presented it as nothing more than a way of "saving the appearances" of the stars and planets and thus a kind of useful fiction, rather than an accurate description of the relationships between the heavenly bodies.

As for Galileo, who during his lifetime did publish his researches confirming Copernicus' cosmology, he discovered how heretical the Church deemed his findings to be and was forced to recant them in order not to be imprisoned or put to death; even so, he was placed under house arrest for the rest of his life. Thus modern science, at its very beginnings, was recognized by the Church as posing a mortal threat to its belief system.

Nietzsche was thus not exaggerating when he attributed both the death of God and the death of morality to the scientific revolution and spoke of "The nihilistic consequences of contemporary natural science ... Since Copernicus man has been rolling from the center toward X."[6]

But long before Nietzsche said it, Shakespeare recognized the practical implications of his statement, for if God is dead, morality is dead, and as Hamlet says, "Nothing is either good or bad but thinking makes it so." Once knowledge is attained not by faith but by restricting belief to those concepts whose truth or falsity can be tested by their consistency with empirical data and evidence, good and evil along with God and the devil give way to observation and experiment. Neither theological nor moral concepts as to what is good or evil can be tested (affirmed or disconfirmed) by empirical tests.

[6] Nietzsche (1968).

Montaigne,[7] one of the major influences on Shakespeare, wrote extensively about the impossibility of attaining moral knowledge, or knowledge of how we should live and what we should do:

> Truth must have one face, the same and universal. If man knew any rectitude and justice that had body and real existence, he would not tie it down to the condition of the customs of this country or that.
>
> There is nothing subject to more continual agitation than the laws. Since I was born I have seen those of our neighbors the English change three or four times; not only in political matters, ... but in the most important subject that can be, to wit, religion.... And here at home I have seen things which were capital offenses among us become legitimate....
>
> What then will philosophy tell us in this our need? To follow the laws of our country – that is to say, the undulating sea of the opinions of a people or a prince, which will paint me justice in as many colors ... as there are changes of passion in those men?
>
> ... What am I to make of a virtue that I saw in credit yesterday, that will be discredited tomorrow, and that becomes a crime on the other side of the river?
>
> ... to give some certainty to the laws, they say that there are some which are firm, perpetual, and immutable, which they call natural, which are imprinted on the human race by the condition of their very being. And of those one man says the number is three, one man four, one more, one less: a sign that the mark of them is as doubtful as the rest.... of these three or four selected laws there is not a single one that is not contradicted and disavowed, not by one nation but by many.
>
> Now the only likely sign by which they can argue certain laws to be natural is universality of approval. For what nature had truly ordered for us we would without doubt follow by common consent. And not only every nation, but every individual, would resent the force and violence used on him by anyone who tried to impel him to oppose that law. Let them show me just one law of that sort – I'd like to see it.
>
> There is nothing in which the world is so varied as in customs and laws. A given thing is abominable here, which brings commendation elsewhere: as in Lacedaemon cleverness in stealing.
>
> ... See how reason provides plausibility to different actions.
>
> The lawyers and judges of our time find enough angles for all cases to arrange them any way they please. In a field ... depending on the authority of so many opinions, and in so arbitrary a subject, it is impossible that there should not arise an extreme confusion of judgments. And so there is hardly a lawsuit so clear that opinions do not differ on it. The judgment one court has given is reversed by another, which reverses itself another time.

---

[7] Montaigne (1965), pp. 435–9.

. . . As for the freedom of philosophical opinions concerning vice and virtue, it is a thing on which there is no need to expand, and on which there are several opinions which are better hushed up than published to weak minds.

The lengthy and multiple descriptions of the subjectivity of moral value judgments by Montaigne that we have just quoted can be summarized much more succinctly by one *New Yorker* cartoon, which we include here.

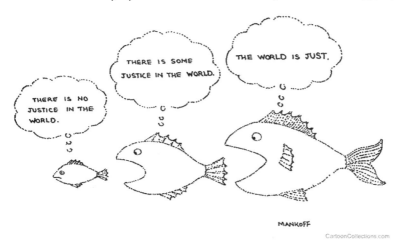

Courtesy of www.cartooncollections.com.

The main difference between Montaigne and Shakespeare on the matter of the loss of credibility of moral value systems is that Shakespeare realized far more clearly than Montaigne ever did, and dramatized in excruciating detail with his character Hamlet, the devastating effect that moral agnosticism, skepticism, and nihilism would have on individuals, and their tragic implications for whole societies. In the character of Hamlet and, more particularly, in his soliloquies, Shakespeare gives voice to the cognitive earthquake created by the revolution of his time.

But Shakespeare was not alone in recognizing this. His contemporary, the poet John Donne, echoes Hamlet in acknowledging the degree to which the scientific revolution had created a "new Philosophy" (meaning Science) that "calls all in doubt," namely, an awareness of the subjectivity, arbitrariness, and lack of credibility of moral value systems, leading to moral nihilism. Here we quote Donne at greater length:[8]

---

[8] John Donne, "An Anatomie of the World" (1611).

> new Philosophy calls all in doubt,
> ... 'Tis all in peeces, all cohaerence gone;
> All just supply, and all Relation;
> Prince, Subject, Father, Son, are things forgot,
> The worlds proportion disfigured is;
> That those two legs whereon it doth rely,
> Reward and punishment are bent awry.
> ... Wicked is not much worse than indiscreet.
> ... All have forgot all good ...

And in another great poem,[9]

> There's nothing simply good, nor ill alone,
> Of every quality Comparison
> The only measure is, and judge, Opinion.

The time, in truth, was out of joint. But not only in Shakespeare and Donne's time, for the problem they described did not disappear. Two centuries later John Stuart Mill was making the same diagnosis of his time: "The first of the leading peculiarities of the present age is, that it is an age of transition. Mankind have outgrown old institutions and old doctrines, and have not yet acquired new ones."[10] This is exactly the problem that paralyzed Hamlet: in the nineteenth century; the time was still out of joint. For as Mill elaborated,

> To have erroneous convictions is one evil; but to have no strong or deep-rooted convictions at all, is an enormous one.... Now, it is self-evident that no fixed opinions have yet generally established themselves in the place of those which we have abandoned; that no new doctrines, philosophical or social, as yet command, or appear likely soon to command, an assent at all comparable in unanimity to that which the ancient doctrines could boast of while they continued in vogue.... [In] this intellectual anarchy ... we have not yet advanced beyond the unsettled state, in which the mind is, when it has recently found itself out in a grievous error, and has not yet satisfied itself of the truth.... here we see the peculiar character, and at the same time the peculiar inconvenience, of a period of moral and social transition. At all other periods there exists a large body of received doctrine, covering nearly the whole field of the moral relations of man, and which no one thinks of questioning, backed as it is by the authority of all ... persons supposed to possess knowledge enough to qualify them for giving an opinion on the subject. This state of things does not now exist in the civilized world.... the old doctrines have gone out, and the new ones have not yet come in.... there must be a change in the whole framework of

---

[9] John Donne, "The Progresse of the Soule" (1601).   [10] Mill (1963), pp. 1–44.

society, as at present constituted.... There must be a moral and social revolution.... man cannot achieve his destiny but through such a transformation.

Later in that same century, Dostoevsky's character, Ivan Karamazov, is paralyzed by the same realization: "Without God, anything is possible, everything is permitted." Without faith in God, faith in morality cannot exist (for both are objects of faith, not knowledge, i.e., confirmation by means of empirical data and evidence).

But what is the alternative?

Again, we return to Hamlet, for this is his question. Are there alternatives to the chaos, nihilism, anarchy, and the sheer paralysis of action that follows from the loss of credibility of the traditional moral belief systems? Or to put it in Hamlet's terms, is there any way of knowing how we should live and what we ought to do? Can we find any terms that are more credible than moral terms for answering the questions raised by practical reason, namely, how to live and what to do?

And here we come to our second realization: Shakespeare was not only the first to recognize how pathological moral nihilism is, he was also the first to show us the alternative. In his plays and with his characters, he both diagnosed the pathology and identified the cure – the cognitive and affective replacements for moral value judgments and commandments.

In the history plays and the tragedies, Shakespeare dramatizes how the moral emotions, shame and guilt, and the moral value systems they inform, shame ethics and guilt ethics, provoke violence and destroy life. In many of the comedies, romances, and so-called problem plays, he shows us the alternatives: love as the *affective* alternative to the moral emotions of shame and guilt, and psychological understanding as the *cognitive* alternative to moral value judgments and commandments, with their condemnations and punishments of self or of others. Morality presumed to tell us how we *should* live, and discovered that it was unable to find an answer to questions put in that way. Psychology has a much humbler and limited goal, which is to answer an empirical question, namely, How *can* we live? In other words, what social and psychological forces and processes tend to cause death, and which ones sustain and maintain life? And that is a question about which it is possible to do research and arrive at answers that are at least credible enough to act on, now that we are in the age of modern science.

What Shakespeare shows us about shame and guilt and love and violence is that love transcends morality, by making it unnecessary and redundant: for when you love, you do not need shame ethics (to command you to benefit yourself) nor guilt ethics (to command you to take care of other people). You spontaneously want to do what those moral value systems would command you to do, so you do not need their commandments: that is what love means. And in the greatest irony of all, morality, whose purpose is ostensibly to prevent or control violence, inhibits love and provokes and justifies violence; shame ethics inhibits the love of others and justifies and even commands hate and violence toward others; and guilt ethics inhibits self-love, and justifies and even commands hate and violence (punishment) toward the self.

Duke Vincentio's fostering of love and his forgiveness of those who would do violence in *Measure for Measure*, Prospero's forgiveness and reconciliation with those who had deposed and exiled him in *The Tempest*, Leontes' restoration of those he had abused and abandoned in *The Winter's Tale* – with these plays Shakespeare dramatizes the rejection of the demands of both a shame ethic and a guilt ethic, and shows us the alternative, namely, repairing and restoring relationships so as to express and achieve reconciliation and love.

As Shakespeare the psychologist makes plain, shame ethics commands hate and in the name of honor justifies murderous violence toward others (as with Othello, Macbeth, Henry V, Richard III, etc.). And guilt ethics commands self-hate and self-murder (as with Othello, Lady Macbeth, Enobarbus, etc.). He also shows us the sources of collective peace or violence in whole cities and states, depending on whether the legal and political institutions and leaders practice restorative or retributive justice. For whereas retributive justice is based on judging others, so as to measure out the quantity of punishment and vengeance that will equal the quantity of evil in their crimes (sometimes literally, as in an eye for an eye, a death for a death), restorative justice operates according to what Abraham Lincoln two centuries later called "malice toward none, charity for all" – which could be seen as the motto of Duke Vincentio.

The Duke's "permissiveness" should not be confused with passivity in the face of actual or potential violence. The Duke does not allow Angelo to kill Claudio. He restrains and prevents him from doing that. But restraint is altogether different from punishment. It harms no one, and merely prevents them from harming anyone else (which, in turn, protects the person who needs to be restrained from provoking others to harm or punish him). When people are actively killing or raping others, we of course need to restrain them, by isolating them from the community until they are no longer dangerous.

But what makes all the difference is what we do with them once we have restrained them in this way. If we offer them something positive – more positive than what they had been given by the families and communities that had raised them, and something with which to repair and reverse the psychological damage that had been done to them by those families and communities – they experience the restraint not as punishment but, rather, as an opportunity for personal growth and healing. For example, one of the violent inmates in the San Francisco violence-prevention experiment, far from wanting to escape from his confinement in the jail, commented with some regret about his pending discharge from the jail: "I should have been in this program for four years, not four months, because I'm trying to change the habits of a lifetime." And, as we said in Chapter 8, the inmates in this program responded to it with feelings not of resentment but of gratitude for what they had learned about themselves – for they had been given something positive and helpful, not punishment and revenge, and they spontaneously wanted to pass on those benefits to new prisoners who were just coming into the jail.

Finally, Shakespeare shows us why people do need to be capable of feeling shame, when that serves the purpose of warning them when they have failed to achieve their full potential for making a positive contribution to their own lives and the lives of others, by developing the knowledge and skills that would enable them to do that: for the failure to do so may limit them to taking advantage of the generosity of others and never learning to take care of themselves and others. The shameless and ambitionless Falstaff exemplifies that, for though he does contribute companionship and friendship to Prince Hal, he nevertheless cannot take care of himself, let alone others, once Hal abandons him.

But the only way in which they can outgrow the conditions that are exposing them to shame by any means other than violence (which itself is only a temporary "fix" that sooner or later reverses itself) is by having access to nonviolent sources of pride and self-esteem – of which education is one of the most effective and efficient, meaning that the benefits are so much greater than the costs. In the mental health program that Gilligan directed in the Massachusetts prisons there was one program, and one only, that was 100 per cent effective in preventing reoffending and reimprisonment, namely, gaining a college degree while in prison. Over a twenty-five-year period, over 200 prisoners, including men who had committed murders, rapes, and other serious violent crimes, earned a bachelor's degree from Boston University, by taking tuition-free courses taught by professors who were donating their time to this project, and not one was reincarcerated for any further criminal activity. The same results have been reported from prisons in many other states. If feeling ignorant and intellectually inferior causes feelings of shame, and shame causes violence, whereas gaining knowledge and skills undoes the feeling of shame, and that prevents violence, these results should hardly be surprising. In fact, they show how shame, and the desire to overcome it, can motivate growth and development and a degree of behavioral capacities that make violence not only unnecessary but undesirable – if access to educational and other nonviolent resources is made available.

Shakespeare also shows us how guilt feelings can serve an adaptive, constructive purpose when they are limited to serving as a "signal anxiety" that one is in danger of harming others. That can indeed inhibit, or decelerate, violent impulses. But that does not limit a person to redirecting the anger that is causing the guilt onto the self. For anger can be put into the service of love – of oneself and of those toward whom one has reason to be angry.

Prospero, for example, serves his own interests (his self-love) by deposing his brother and undoing the King of Naples' partnership in that crime, and achieving the restoration of his dukedom (a good example of "restorative" justice). In so doing he has committed no violence against anyone. And he has removed the very cause of whatever anger he felt toward those who had been his enemies (what today would be called the "downward social mobility" that they had subjected him to, which causes shame), and thus removed the very thing that causes guilt feelings – namely, anger. With the causes of his anger removed, he has no need to waste his time and energy pursuing retribution and revenge by punishing his former enemies (who are now no longer his enemies) – for nothing constructive, for him or for them, would be accomplished by that. And with the causes of guilt feelings removed, he has no motivation to harm or punish himself. He has not only undone his enemies' aggression against him; he has also restrained them from harming (even killing) each other. And he has achieved a further guarantee of a peaceful future among all of them by blessing the wedding of the King's son to his own daughter – a wedding that was, incidentally, not one that was imposed on that couple by their parents for dynastic reasons, though it did indeed serve those interests. This was a wedding that the two desired for their own reasons, because of their love for each other.

What Prospero did should not be confused with Lady Macbeth's strategy for minimizing and neutralizing guilt feelings. She anesthetized Macbeth's guilt feelings, not by redirecting his murderous impulses toward

Duncan into the service of love but by overpowering his capacity for feelings of guilt by bombarding him with their opposites and antagonists, feelings of shame. For she recognized that any guilt feelings on his part would inhibit him from committing murder. For both of them, timely guilt feelings could have saved not only the lives of others, but their own lives as well, if they had put their guilt feelings to rest by putting their violent impulses and anger into the service of love.

What adds to our confidence in the psychological validity and authenticity of Shakespeare's depictions of both violent and nonviolent people, and of the causes and prevention of violence, is that his imagined characters match so accurately myriad actual people that I (James Gilligan) have seen over the past fifty years, in prisons and courtrooms in this country and around the world, from those who were murderous and suicidal to those who were actively preventing violence. As described earlier in this book, I have seen Othello, Timon, Richard III, Edmund, and many others, many times each. I have been Hamlet myself, in the sense of wrestling with his moral perplexities (but fortunately, not in his life-and-death circumstances). And I have seen Duke Vincentio in the sheriff and program director of the San Francisco jails, and two judges in Boston, all of whom sponsored restorative justice programs, rather than using their power to inflict pain on a (literally) captive audience.

Shakespeare matches the description Aristotle made of tragic poetry, which justifies our calling him the first psychologist of the modern era, when he wrote that

> a poet's object is not to tell what actually happened but what could and would happen either probably or inevitably. The difference between a historian and a poet is . . . that one tells what happened and the other what might happen. For this reason poetry is something more scientific and serious than history, because poetry tends to give general truths while history gives particular facts. By a "general truth" I mean the sort of thing that a certain type of man will do or say either probably or necessarily. (Aristotle, *Poetics*, IX.1–10)

By those criteria, Shakespeare's "imagined" characters may be seen as deserving of as much or more respect and study, as examples of psychological science, as the case histories of actual individuals in today's clinics and prisons, or those in the custody of the World Court in the Hague who are being tried for war crimes. In any case, we believe that we in America, and indeed in the world as a whole, have much to learn, which we need to learn, from the study of Shakespeare's plays, not only about the causes and prevention of individual violence but, much more importantly, about collective political violence. For many of today's world's leaders, and their followers and supporters, are just as much examples of shame-driven personalities as Macbeth, Henry V, Richard III, Coriolanus, or many others among Shakespeare's large cast of political mass murderers. And unfortunately, they have technologies at their disposal that are incomparably more deadly than any that were at the disposal even of Shakespeare's most homicidal leaders.

Today's political leaders usually delegate the actual slaughtering of whole cities to their underlings, just as Henry V did, which actually makes them more dangerous, not less, than the individual murderers whom the criminal justice system focuses on. What is relevant here, however, is that by noticing which leaders are most shame-driven, we can identify those who are most dangerous even before they have provoked and incited millions of murders, among whom are the panoply of politicians who have attained dictatorial power in an increasing number of countries across the globe – and who nearly did (and may yet do) in the United States.[11] Since many of those leaders have a stockpile of thermonuclear weapons at their disposal, the scale of violence they are capable of committing – just by giving an order – is unprecedented and unimaginable.

Those are among the reasons we feel that it is so important for us to learn from Shakespeare and understand what he has shown us. We know that Hitler wound up being a modern version of Timon of Athens. But we also know that new dictators are coming to power in country after country, throughout the world, with the potential to kill incomparably more people than even the deadliest of the twentieth-century tyrants. Shakespeare described a world without democracy, and we are living in a world of shrinking and imperiled democracy. To say that he is our contemporary is not just a slogan. It is the literal truth.

To sum up: Shakespeare, the first and still greatest psychologist of the modern (post-Medieval) era, shows us in his plays the psychological evidence –the detailed thoughts, feelings, and actions of his characters – that can be summarized and paraphrased in theoretical terms as three great discoveries. The first is the causes of violence, toward others or toward the self, respectively, namely, the opposite and antagonistic moral emotions of shame and guilt. Shakespeare shows how shame motivates self-love, or egoism (since it consists of a deficiency of self-love, i.e., a narcissistic injury), and hatred toward others, as shown by Richard III,

---

11 Gilligan (2017).

Henry V, Iago, Othello, Macbeth, Edmund, Timon, and many others; whereas guilt motivates self-hate (self-condemnation, self-punishment, even self-murder), and love of others – as shown by Othello, Enobarbus, et al. These emotions motivate two opposite moral codes, shame ethics and guilt ethics; the character structures built around those moral codes: shame-driven versus guilt-ridden personalities (e.g., Richard III and Henry V vs. Henry VI and Enobarbus, respectively); and the shame or guilt cultures whose ethos consists of one or the other of those two moral value systems (e.g., the shame culture represented by Hamlet's father's ghost, with its call for revenge, vs. the guilt culture represented by the literal, official, though often ignored commandments of the Christian religion, for the forgiveness and love of one's enemies, and self-punishment for one's own sins). The most radical implication of this discovery is that morality, which is usually considered as the ultimate means of preventing violence, is actually the cause of both forms of violence: shame ethics, of violence toward others (as in homicide and war), and sometimes of oneself as well (as in apocalyptic violence, or suicides committed in order to end unavoidable humiliations); and guilt ethics, of violence toward the self (as in suicides committed in order to inhibit or prevent violence toward others).

The second great discovery that Shakespeare represents on the stage is the recognition that because of the scientific revolution occurring at the time in which he was writing, when the faith-based mentality of the Medieval era was being replaced by the doubt-based mentality of modernity and the modern mind, both moral codes lost their credibility, since knowledge (objectivity) was possible only by means of empirical verification, that is, facts; whereas values, being subjective, could not be verified by those means. As Hamlet put it, "there is nothing either good or bad but thinking makes it so." That awareness of the subjectivity and arbitrariness of what had previously been thought to be objectively true, independently of human beings and their thoughts, destroyed the credibility not just of God and the devil but also of good and evil – meaning the credibility of *both* moral value systems, which created a vacuum in the sphere of practical reason that we call moral nihilism. And as the life and death of Hamlet, who has been called the first modern personality, exemplifies, moral nihilism creates behavioral paralysis and is therefore incompatible with ongoing life.

The third great discovery that Shakespeare showed us in the form of stories (one of which, in *Measure for Measure*, is the equivalent of a scientific psychological experiment yielding empirical data) is that violence can be prevented, when we transcend the moral emotions of shame (which inhibits the love of others) and guilt (which inhibits self-love, or pride) with the capacity for love of both self and others; and thereby replace "retributive justice" (moral condemnation and punishment of self or others) with "restorative justice." That latter concept would more accurately be termed the transcendence of justice and morality altogether, and the replacement of the moral affects and cognitive structures with the affect of love (of both self and others), and the cognitive/psychological understanding of the causes and prevention of violence.

That point of view would suggest responding to violence not as a moral problem but as a problem in public health, which creates death and disability on as large a scale as the deadliest epidemics of disease, and therefore requires emphasizing prevention before it has occurred, rather than punishment after the victims are already dead. For the combination of love and psychological understanding motivates us to do what morality would command us to do toward those we love anyway, and thus makes both systems of moral value judgments and commandments (shame ethics and guilt ethics) unnecessary and redundant – as exemplified by Duke Vincentio, Prospero, the major protagonists in *The Winter's Tale*, and many others.

Those plays illustrate attitudes and practices that prevent violence both by private individuals and by the state. They allow reconciliation between offenders and their victims, thus restoring the sense of safety and trust to the victims and the community at large, which the offenders had taken from them. And they restore to offenders the freedom to live in the community, which may have had to be taken from them until they could learn to renounce violence as their means of expressing their feelings and pursuing their goals. In today's criminal justice system, this is represented by advocates of restorative justice, "therapeutic jurisprudence," specialized courts for people suffering from drug addictions or mental illnesses, and many other policy recommendations whose purpose is the prevention of violence, rather than the infliction of it by the state (which is called "retributive justice").

We have been guided throughout this book by the continuing rediscovery of how astonishingly Shakespeare's delineation of the detailed thoughts, feelings, and actions of his characters precisely parallels the corresponding phenomena in the violent people and groups (mostly men) whom we have observed in our own time. Learning what we can from Shakespeare thus appears to us as vitally helpful, in our effort to prevent the escalation of violence from the genocides that have repeatedly occurred throughout the past hundred years to the apocalyptic violence that our current technologies, which are themselves the products of the explosive growth in our scientific knowledge over the past century, have made possible. For what we have now brought on ourselves is irreversible: it is the ever-present potential, and therefore danger, of making us the first species in the history of evolution to render itself extinct by means of its own self-destructive behavior, rather than because of changes in the environment beyond its capacity to control. Since it is too late to unlearn the means for making both thermonuclear weapons and the fossil-fuel energy technologies that are destroying the viability of our planet, we can only hope that it is not too late for us to learn what makes those weapons and technologies seem necessary and irreplaceable, so that we can also learn how to remove or neutralize the social and psychological conditions that motivate people to kill each other and themselves.

Acknowledgments

Our work on this book arose from our co-teaching an interdisciplinary seminar at the New York University School of Law, "Retribution in Criminal Justice," in the course of which Jim and I (David Richards) began discussing Jim's long-standing view that in his work as a psychiatrist with violent criminals Shakespeare's plays had been helpful if not indispensable in understanding how and why the men he dealt with could have committed violence on the scale and degree of destructiveness with which they had done so. On the basis of our discussions, we refocused the seminar in the past three years on what Shakespeare showed us about violence and its relation to manhood, discussing with our students our developing views, reflected in the first drafts of this book. All the students in these three seminars made an invaluable contribution to our arguments, several of whom we explicitly acknowledge in our argument. We are grateful to all of them, and want to acknowledge them here. Accordingly, we thank, in the first year we gave the seminar: Katherine Natasha Adams, Stav Cohen, Katherine Elizabeth Coric, Olga Anna Kosno, Michael Lessard, Elena Hull Nichols, Angelica Puzio, Bomi Sohn, Nithya Swaminathan, Daniela Ugaz, and Zhongji Wu; and, in the second year, Laura Dorith A. Adriaensens, Eun-Bit Chang, Lana Dziekonski, Isaac Fink, Timothy Haase, Catherine Larsen, Nicholas C. Lee-Wunderlich, Alicia M. Morejon, Shivani I. Morrison, Rebecca E. Pritzker, Oren Stevens, Karis E. Stubblefield, and Gary Richard Uter; and, in the third year, Lillian Cowan, Eryn Hughes, Frank Joranko, Lucas Knoll, Asha McLachlan, Esteban Ochoa, and Ahmed Tarek Yacout Saleh.

I had taught a seminar, "Resisting Injustice," with Carol Gilligan for the past twenty years (coauthoring two books together), and it was through her that Jim and I met and began teaching together. Throughout our work together, Carol has been an invaluable interlocutor and guide, including reading and commenting on our drafts. We would not have written this book without her loving, caring presence in both our lives.

My work on the psychology of love was illuminated by continuing conversations with Phillip Blumberg, who guided me through the psychoanalytic and related literatures, and with my life partner, Donald Levy, whose papers on Plato on love and the unnatural as a moral category were invaluable. I also must thank Lavinia Barbu, my assistant, for service above and beyond the call of duty preparing the bibliography for this book.

The research and writing of this book during the summers was supported in part by generous grants from the New York University School of Law Filomen D'Agostino and Max E. Greenberg Faculty Research Fund. We are grateful as well for the support of the law school dean, Trevor Morrison, as well as the faculty of the NYU School of Law for supporting interdisciplinary work of this kind and for their comments on our argument in a faculty workshop. And we thank as well David Repetto, our editor at Cambridge, as well as the excellent readers he secured.

David A. J. Richards

In acknowledging those who have contributed to whatever we have achieved in this book, I (James Gilligan) cannot begin to mention more than a few – there have been so many. I will begin by acknowledging one of my primary debts in this book to the late Professor Harry Levin, with whom I studied Shakespeare at Harvard College, and whose influence on my thinking about *Hamlet* became clear to me only when I reviewed my notes from years past in preparation for this book. My thinking about shame and guilt was facilitated by discussions with the psychologist Daniel Levinson, a coauthor of *The Authoritarian Personality*; the sociologist David Riesman, with whom I spent a year as his research assistant, during which he reviewed and generously encouraged my own research on the psychology and sociology of shame and guilt; the psychoanalyst Erich Fromm, who offered thoughtful responses to my work on shame, guilt, violence, and authoritarianism, in the light of his own writings on those subjects, when he visited Riesman several times during the year I worked with him; and the cardiologist Dr. Bernard Lown, with whom I spent a year as a research assistant at the Harvard Schools of Public Health and of Medicine, during which he founded Physicians for Social Responsibility, and then expanded it into International Physicians for the Prevention of Nuclear War (later awarded the 1985 Nobel Peace Prize), which showed me that medical knowledge was relevant, and could be applied, to the problem of political violence. He was certainly the most important, valuable, and relevant mentor and inspiration I had, not only for the writing of this book but for my career as a whole.

Dr. Douglas Bond, the Dean of the Medical School of Western Reserve University (and former head of psychiatric services for the US Air Force in England during World War II), reviewed and encouraged my work on the psychology, sociology, and anthropology of shame and guilt, and their relationship to paranoia and depression, respectively, on which I wrote my MD thesis. Dr. Gerald Adler gave me my first opportunity to engage violent prison inmates in psychotherapy, in addition to leading a seminar on the psychology of violence, during my residency training in psychiatry at the Harvard Medical School. I was privileged to spend many evenings discussing psychoanalytic theory and its application to historical figures such as Luther, Hitler, and Gandhi with the psychoanalyst Erik Erikson, after I was invited to give the Erikson Lectures at Harvard University on shame, guilt, and the causes and prevention of violence.

During two years I spent as a Visiting Fellow at the Institute of Criminology at the University of Cambridge I was blessed by the opportunity to establish relationships with four brilliant and innovative psychiatrists who inspired much of my later work. The first was the late (and deeply lamented) Dr. Murray Cox, who was doing much the same kind of work in England's main psychiatric prison hospital for the violent mentally ill (the "criminally insane"), Broadmoor Hospital, as I had done in the corresponding institution, the Bridgewater State Hospital, in Massachusetts. He showed me a way to combine two interests we shared, in linking the work of Shakespeare to the understanding of violence – though he did so much more dramatically than I had ever done, by inviting members of the Royal Shakespeare Company to perform plays of Shakespeare for the patients at Broadmoor. He also joined with another Shakespeare lover, Rowan Williams, who was then the Archbishop of Wales, in founding a group meeting for a long weekend once every other year, to have a "Trialogue," a group discussion of specified works of literature, psychoanalysis, and theology, and the relevance of these three disciplines to each other – during which I was able to learn a great deal from discussions of my own work and that of others.

The second was Dr. Estela Welldon, who had the creativity and initiative to construct an unprecedented training program for mental health professionals in the understanding and treatment of violent offenders, at the Portman Clinic of the Tavistock Institute, and founded a group I joined and later served as president for, the International Association for Forensic Psychotherapy. The third was Dr. Adrian

Grounds, a member of the faculty of Cambridge's Institute of Criminology, who performed insightful forensic psychiatric evaluations that were crucial in ameliorating the judicial, penal, and psychiatric disposition of imprisoned combatants during the "Troubles" in Northern Ireland, and who was very generous in sharing his insights with me. The fourth was Dr. John Alderdice, whose skill in applying psychoanalytic understanding to political conflicts made a significant contribution to the attainment of peace in Northern Ireland, which is why he is now Lord Alderdice. I also benefited from the good offices of Anthony, Lord Lloyd, who invited me, together with Drs. Grounds and Welldon, to spend a weekend with himself and other Law Lords in Windsor Great Park discussing the application of psychiatric and psychoanalytic knowledge to the causes and prevention of violence, from which I learned much about the practices of the criminal justice system in the United Kingdom (and their superiority to many of those in effect in the United States). Anthony Giddens, who was then a professor of sociology at the University of Cambridge, added crucial components to my knowledge about modernity, morality, and violence, and enabled me to (temporarily) dissuade Tony Blair, then the "shadow" Home Secretary, from repeating the mistakes of the American penal system.

I am also indebted to the late Nancy Paterson, a member of the prosecutorial staff of the International Criminal Tribunal for the former Yugoslavia in the Hague, for inviting me to help her and her colleagues to persuade the World Court (the International Court of Justice) to prosecute the systematic mass rapes that were occurring in the Balkan wars of the 1990s and elsewhere as war crimes and crimes against humanity, rather than merely as random, individual crimes of rape. Alexander Butchart and Etienne Krug, of the Department of Injuries and Violence Prevention of the World Health Organization in Geneva, by inviting me to be a consultant and lecturer to their staff, enabled me to participate in multiple meetings around the world, both teaching and learning from individuals and groups who were attempting to prevent violence on a worldwide basis. A similar invitation from the World Economic Forum enabled me to deliver lectures, participate in panel discussions, and become a member of their Committee on Negotiations and Conflict Resolution, in meetings throughout the world, from which I learned more about the causes and prevention of political violence than I could ever have learned on my own.

I owe a special debt to two lawyers, Michael Hennessey, who was then the sheriff of the City and County of San Francisco, and his program director, Sunny Schwartz, who as I say in Chapter 8 of this book were reincarnations of Duke Vincentio, by virtue of their inviting me to design an experimental test of the hypothesis that restorative justice would be more effective in preventing violence than retributive justice was (a project that would have been impossible without the indefatigable data collection and analysis of my research partner, Dr. Bandy Lee). And I want to thank the two other now deceased heroes who in my experience also qualify as reincarnations of the Duke in *Measure for Measure*, namely, Judge W. Arthur Garrity of the US District Court in Boston and G. Joseph Tauro, chief justice of the Massachusetts Supreme Court, both of whom ordered the state of Massachusetts to allow a team of mental health professionals from the Harvard Medical School into the state's prisons and prison mental hospital, respectively, in order to replace retributive justice with restorative justice, which made it possible for me to increase my understanding of how to prevent violence and how to enable the men in those institutions to become restored to, and reconciled with, their communities.

A particular debt is owed to my friend and colleague Tina Packer, the brilliant English American cofounder and artistic director of Shakespeare and Company, the repertory theater company devoted to productions of his plays in Lenox, MA, who has served not only as a constant source of insights into Shakespeare's achievement but as director of an intensive month-long workshop for actors which I participated in, which gave me the opportunity to explore the "mind of the murderer" with an intensity and specificity that I could never have achieved on my own, in casting me as Othello in the murder scene of that tragedy. I also learned from an actor and director who was then with that company, Brent Blair (who now does the same thing as a professor at the University of Southern California), who engaged members of violent youth gangs in Boston as actors in productions of Shakespeare's plays. When they performed excerpts from *Hamlet* before the students in a class Carol Gilligan taught at Harvard's Graduate School of Education, one of them commented how he had never realized how words – Shakespeare's words – could have the power to express emotions so powerfully that he did not need violent actions to do the same thing.

I do wish to acknowledge the contribution that Trevor Morrison, the dean of the law school of New York University, made to the writing of this book when he invited David and me to present a preview of it to the entire law school faculty, followed by a discussion which he moderated, during which we received especially helpful, indeed invaluable, comments from our old and good friends and distinguished colleagues, Moshe Halbertal and Stephen Holmes.

I also need to acknowledge the gift, and the example, my three sons have given me (respectively), in engaging in multidisciplinary approaches to reducing the violence against our environment that are rapidly making our world uninhabitable (Jonathan); improving physicians' abilities to communicate with and respond to the needs of their patients, in addition to (though it is actually an intrinsic component of) curing their illnesses (Timothy); and reducing the amount of pain patients are experiencing, regardless of their medical diagnosis (Christopher). All of them are working as hard as I am to solve the equivalent of the same problems that I am attempting to find solutions for in this book.

Finally, I want to acknowledge the unique contributions of Carol Gilligan to many of the editorial and stylistic issues faced in the writing of this book (and in my life). Without her invaluable help, I could never have written it (or lived) as I have. Whatever misstatements or omissions still exist are my responsibility alone. I can only acknowledge that there would have been many more without her loving help.

James Gilligan

Bibliography

Adorno, Theodor W., Else Frenkel-Brunswick, Daniel J. Levinson, and R. Nevitt Sanford, *The Authoritarian Personality* (New York: Harper & Row, 1950).

Altemeyer, Bob, *Right-Wing Authoritarianism* (Manitoba, Canada: University of Manitoba Press, 1981).

The Authoritarian Specter (Cambridge, MA: Harvard University Press, 1996).

Ayers, Edward L., *Vengeance and Justice: Crime and Punishment in the 19th-Century American South* (New York: Oxford University Press, 1984).

Baker, Herschel, footnote to *Henry V*, in G. Blakemore Evans (ed.), *The Riverside Shakespeare* (Boston, MA: Houghton Mifflin, 1974), p. 971.

Barbu, Zevedei, *Problems of Historical Psychology* (New York: Grove Press, 1960).

Barton, Anne, *Troilus and Cressida*, in G. Blakemore Evans (ed.), *The Riverside Shakespeare* (Boston, MA: Houghton Mifflin, 1974).

Benedict, Ruth, *The Chrysanthemum and the Sword: Patterns of Japanese Culture* (Boston, MA: Houghton Mifflin, 1946).

"The Northwest Coast of America," in *Patterns of Culture* (New York: New American Library, 1958), pp. 173–222.

Bloom, Harold, *Shakespeare: The Invention of the Human* (New York: Riverhead Books, 1998).

Boas, Franz, *Kwakiutl Ethnography*, ed. Helen Codere (Chicago, IL: University of Chicago Press, 1966).

Butterfield, Herbert, *The Origins of Modern Science, 1300–1800* (New York: Macmillan, 1959).

Buttrick, David, *Speaking Jesus: Homiletic Theology and the Sermon on the Mount* (Louisville, KY: Westminster John Knox Press, 2002).

Coleridge, Samuel Taylor, *Lectures on Shakespeare (1811–1819)*, ed. Adam Roberts (Edinburgh: Edinburgh University Press, 2016).

Collingwood, R. G., *The Idea of History* (Oxford: Oxford University Press, 1994).

Cox, Murray (ed.), *Shakespeare Comes to Broadmoor: "The Actors Come Hither"* (London: Jessica Kingsley, 1992).

De Rougemont, Denis, *Love in the Western World*, (Princeton, NJ: Princeton University Press, 1983).

Dodds, Eric R., *The Greeks and the Irrational* (Berkeley, CA: University of California Press, 1951).

Donne, John, "An Anatomie of the World" (1611), in *The Poems of John Donne*, ed. Sir Herbert Grierson (London: Oxford University Press, 1951).

"The Progresse of the Soule" (1601), in *The Poems of John Donne*, ed. Sir Herbert Grierson (London: Oxford University Press, 1951).

Eaton, Joseph, and Robert J. Weil, *Culture and Mental Disorders: A Comparative Study of the Hutterites and Other Populations* (Glencoe, IL: Free Press, 1955).

Evans, G. Blakemore (ed.), *The Riverside Shakespeare* (Boston, MA: Houghton Mifflin, 1974).

Febvre, Lucien, *The Problem of Unbelief in the Sixteenth Century: The Religion of Rabelais* (Cambridge, MA.: Harvard University Press, 1982 [1942]).

Fenichel, Otto, *The Psychoanalytic Theory of Neurosis* (New York: W. W. Norton, 1945).

Ferguson, Robert A., *Inferno: An Anatomy of American Punishment* (Cambridge, MA: Harvard University Press, 2014).

Freud, Sigmund, "Some Character-Types Met with in Psychoanalytic Work," in *The Standard Edition of the Complete Psychological Works of Sigmund Freud*, vol. 14 (1914–16) (London: Hogarth Press, 1957).

"Civilization and Its Discontents," in *The Standard Edition of the Complete Psychological Works of Sigmund Freud*, vol. 21 (1927–31) (London: Hogarth Press, 1961).

"Studies on Hysteria," in *The Standard Edition of the Psychological Works of Sigmund Freud*, trans. James Strachey, vol. 2 (1893–5) (London: Hogarth Press, 1973).

Gilligan, Carol, *The Birth of Pleasure: A New Map of Love* (New York: Knopf, 2002).

Joining the Resistance (Cambridge: Polity Press, 2011).

Gilligan, Carol, and David A. J. Richards, *The Deepening Darkness: Patriarchy, Resistance, and Democracy's Future* (Cambridge: Cambridge University Press, 2009).

Darkness Now Visible: Patriarchy's Resurgence and Feminist Resistance (Cambridge: Cambridge University Press, 2018).

Gilligan, James, "Beyond Morality: Psychoanalytic Reflections on Shame, Guilt and Love," in Thomas Lickona (ed.), *Moral Development and Behavior: Theory, Research and Social Issues* (New York: Holt, Rinehart and Winston, 1975), pp. 144–58.

Violence: Our Deadly Epidemic and Its Causes (New York: Grosset/Putnam, 1996).

"Psychological Violence," in Ronald Gottesman (ed.), *Violence in America: An Encyclopedia*, vol. 2 (New York: Charles Scribner's Sons, 1999), pp. 626–31.

"Punishment and Violence: Is the Criminal Justice System Based on One Huge Mistake?," *Social Research* 67(3) (2000): 745–72.

"Terrorism, Fundamentalism and Nihilism: Analyzing the Dilemmas of Modernity," in Henri Parens and Stuart Twemlow (eds.), *The Future of Prejudice: Applications of Psychoanalytic Understanding toward Its Prevention* (New York: Rowman & Littlefield, 2006).

"Introduction," in Sunny Schwartz (with David Boodell), *Dreams from the Monster Factory: A Tale of Prison, Redemption and One Woman's Fight to Restore Justice to All* (New York: Scribner, 2009), pp. xiii–xx.

"Sex, Gender and Violence," *British Journal of Psychotherapy*, 25(2) (2009): 239–56.

"A Modest Proposal to Universalize the Insanity Defense and Replace Prisons and Punishment with Treatment and Education," *International Journal of Applied Psychoanalytic Studies*, 12(2) (2015): 134–42.

"Can Psychoanalysis Help Us to Understand the Causes and Prevention of Violence?" *Psychoanalytic Psychotherapy*, 30(2) (May 2016): 125–37.

"The Issue Is Dangerousness, Not Mental Illness," in Bandy Lee (ed.), *The Dangerous Case of Donald Trump* (New York: St. Martin's Press, 2017), pp. 170–80.

"Toward a Psychoanalytic Theory of Violence, Fundamentalism and Terrorism," *International Forum of Psychoanalysis*, 26(3) (2017): 174–85.

"Violence," in Salman Akhtar and Stuart Twemlow (eds.), *Textbook of Applied Psychoanalysis* (London: Karnac Books, 2018).

"Violence, Morality and Religion," *Tikkun*, 33(4) (Fall 2018): 49–61.

"Why We Should Universalize the Insanity Defense and Replace Punishment with Therapy and Education," *Aggression and Violent Behavior*, 46 (May 2019): 225–31.

"Punishment, Shaming and Violence," in Farah Focquaert, Elizabeth Shaw, and Bruce Waller (eds.), *Routledge Handbook of the Philosophy and Practice of Punishment* (New York: Routledge, 2021).

Gilligan, James, and Bandy Lee, "Beyond the Prison Paradigm: From Provoking Violence to Preventing It by Creating 'Anti-Prisons' (Residential Colleges and Therapeutic Communities," *Annals of the New York Academy of Sciences*, 1036 (2004): 300–24.

"The Resolve to Stop the Violence Project: Reducing Violence in the Community through a Jail-Based Initiative," *Journal of Public Health*, 27 (2) (June 2005): 143–8.

Gilmore, David D. (ed.), *Honor and Shame and the Unity of the Mediterranean* (Washington, DC: American Anthropological Association, 1987).

Manhood in the Making: Cultural Concepts of Masculinity (New Haven, CT: Yale University Press, 1990).

Gottesman, Ronald, and James Gilligan (eds.), *Violence in America: An Encyclopedia*, 3 vols. (New York: Charles Scribner's Sons, 1999).

Greenblatt, Stephen, *Tyrant: Shakespeare on Politics* (New York: W. W. Norton, 2018).

Hartmann, Heinz, *Psychoanalysis and Moral Values* (New York: International Universities Press, 1960).

Hostetler, John A., and Gertrude E. Huntington, *The Hutterites in North America* (New York: Holt, Rinehart and Winston, 1967).

Hume, David, *A Treatise of Human Nature: Being an Attempt to Introduce the Experimental Method of Reasoning into Moral Subjects*, ed. L. A. Selby-Bigge (Oxford: Clarendon Press, 1951 [1888]).

An Enquiry Concerning the Principles of Morals, 3rd ed., ed. L. A. Selby-Bigge, with text revised by P. H. Nidditch (Oxford: Clarendon Press, 1975).

Jaeger, Werner, *Paideia: The Ideals of Greek Culture, vol. 1: Archaic Greece/The Mind of Athens*, 2nd ed., trans. Gilbert Highet (New York: Oxford University Press, 1965).

Kant, Immanuel, "Of the Motives of Pure Practical Reason," in *The Critique of Practical Reason*, Part I, Book I, Chapter III (Chicago, IL: Encyclopaedia Brittanica, 1952).

Kaplan, Bert, and Thomas F. A. Plaut, *Personality in a Communal Society: Analysis of the Mental Health of the Hutterites* (Lawrence, KS: University of Kansas Press, 1956).

Kohut, Heinz, *The Analysis of the Self: A Systematic Approach to the Psychoanalytic Treatment of Narcissistic Personality Disorders* (Chicago, IL: University of Chicago Press, 1971).

The Restoration of the Self (New York: International Universities Press, 1977).

Lee, Bandy, and James Gilligan, "The Resolve to Stop the Violence Project: Transforming an In-House Culture of Violence through a Jail-Based Programme," *Journal of Public Health*, 27(2) (June 2005): 149–55.

Levin, Harry, *The Question of Hamlet* (New York: Oxford University Press, 1959).

Shakespeare and the Revolution of the Times (New York: Oxford University Press, 1976).

Lipset, Seymour Martin, "Working-Class Authoritarianism," in *Political Man* (New York: Doubleday, 1960).

Lorenz, Konrad, *On Aggression* (New York: Harcourt Brace Jovanovich, 1974).

Mill, John Stuart, "The Spirit of the Age," *Examiner*, January 6–May 29, 1831; reprinted in *Essays on Politics and Culture*, ed. and with an introduction by Gertrude Himmelfarb (New York: Anchor Books, 1963), pp. 1–44.

Montaigne, "Apology for Raymond Sebond," Essays II.12 in *The Complete Essays of Montaigne*, trans. Donald M. Frame (Stanford, CA: Stanford University Press, 1965).

Morrison, Andrew P. (ed.), *Essential Papers on Narcissism* (New York: New York University Press, 1986).

Nietzsche, Friedrich, "Beyond Good and Evil," in *Basic Writings of Nietzsche* (New York: Modern Library, 1968), pp. 181–438.

The Will to Power (New York: Vintage Books, 1968).

On the Genealogy of Morals (Cambridge: Cambridge University Press, 2004).

Onions, C. T., *A Shakespeare Glossary*, enlarged and revised by Robert D. Eagleson (Oxford: Clarendon Press, 1986).

Packer, Tina, *Women of Will: Following the Feminine in Shakespeare's Plays* (New York: Alfred A. Knopf, 2015).

Palmer, Stuart, *A Study of Murder* (New York: Thomas Y. Crowell, 1960).

Piaget, Jean, *The Moral Judgment of the Child* (New York: Free Press, 1965 [1934]).

Piers, Gerhart, and Milton B. Singer, *Shame and Guilt: A Psychoanalytic and a Cultural Study* (New York: W. W. Norton, 1971).

Pitt-Rivers, Julian, "Honor and Social Status," in J. G. Peristiany (ed.), *Honour and Shame: The Values of Mediterranean Society* (Chicago, IL: University of Chicago Press, 1966), pp. 19–77.

   "Honor," in David L. Sills (ed.), *International Encyclopedia of Social Science* (New York: Macmillan, 1968), pp. 503–11.

Reichenbach, Hans, *The Rise of Scientific Philosophy* (Berkeley, CA: University of California Press, 1951).

Richards, David A. J., *A Theory of Reasons for Action* (Oxford: Clarendon Press, 1971).

   Sex, Drugs, Death and the Law: An Essay on Human Rights and Overcriminalization (Totowa, NJ: Rowman and Littlefield, 1982).

   Foundations of American Constitutionalism (New York: Oxford University Press, 1989).

   Toleration and the Constitution (New York: Oxford University Press, 1989).

   Conscience and the Constitution: History, Theory, and Law of the Reconstruction Amendments (Princeton, NJ: Princeton University Press, 1993).

   Women, Gays, and the Constitution: The Grounds for Feminism and Gay Rights in Culture and Law (Chicago, IL: University of Chicago Press, 1998).

   Free Speech and the Politics of Identity (Oxford: Oxford University Press, 1999).

   Identity and the Case for Gay Rights: Race, Gender, Religion as Analogies (Chicago, IL: University of Chicago Press, 1999).

   Italian American: The Racializing of an Ethnic Identity (New York: New York University Press, 1999).

   Tragic Manhood and Democracy: Verdi's Voice and the Powers of Musical Art (Brighton: Sussex Academic Press, 2004).

   Disarming Manhood: Roots of Ethical Resistance (Athens, OH: Swallow Press, 2005).

   (with Nicholas Bamforth), *Patriarchal Religion, Sexuality, and Gender: A Critique of New Natural Law* (Cambridge: Cambridge University Press, 2008).

   Fundamentalism in American Religion and Law: Obama's Challenge to Patriarchy's Threat to Democracy (Cambridge: Cambridge University Press, 2010).

   Resisting Injustice and the Feminist Ethics of Care in the Age of Obama: "Suddenly, . . . All the Truth Was Coming Out" (New York: Routledge, 2013).

   The Rise of Gay Rights and the Fall of the British Empire (New York: Cambridge University Press, 2013).

   Why Love Leads to Justice: Love across the Boundaries (New York: Cambridge University Press, 2016).

   Boys' Secrets and Men's Loves: A Memoir (Bloomington, IN: Ex Libris, 2019).

Rosaldo, Michelle, "The Shame of Headhunters and the Autonomy of Self," *Ethos: Journal of the Society for Psychological Anthropology*, 11(3) (Fall 1983): 135–51.

Roueche, Berton, "The Prognosis for This Patient Is Horrible," *New Yorker*, January 17, 1982.

Schwartz, Sunny (with David Boodell), *Dreams from the Monster Factory*, introduction by James Gilligan (New York: Scribner, 2009).

Shengold, Leonard, *Soul Murder: The Effects of Childhood Abuse and Deprivation* (New Haven, CT: Yale University Press, 1989).

Shirer, William L., *The Rise and Fall of the Third Reich: A History of Nazi Germany* (New York: Simon and Schuster, 1960).

Silberman, Charles E., *Criminal Violence, Criminal Justice* (New York: Random House, 1978).

Slater, Philip E., and Dori A. Slater, "Maternal Ambivalence and Narcissism: A Cross-Cultural Study," *Merrill-Palmer Quarterly of Behavior and Development*, 11(3) (July 1965): 241–59.

Stendhal, *On Love* (London: Hesperus Press, 2009 [1822]).

Strindberg, August, "Soul Murder" [1887], *Drama Review*, 13 (1968): 113–18.

Textor, Robert B., *A Cross-Cultural Summary* (New Haven, CT: Human Relations Area Files Press, 1972).

Tomkins, Silvan S., "Ideology and Affect" and "The Socialization of Affect," in E. Virginia Demos (ed.), *Exploring Affect: The Selected Writings of Silvan S. Tomkins* (Cambridge: Cambridge University Press, 1995), pp. 109–95.

Veblen, Thorstein, "Christian Morals and the Competitive System," *International Journal of Ethics*, 20(2) (January 1910): 168–85.

  The Theory of the Leisure Class: An Economic Study of Institutions, the Mentor Edition, introduction by C. Wright Mills (New York: Macmillan, 1953 [1899]).

Whitehead, Alfred North, *Science and the Modern World* (New York: Mentor, 1948 [1925]).

Woolf, Virginia, *Three Guineas* (New York: Harcourt, Brace and Jovanovich, 1966 [1938]).

Wyatt-Brown, Bertram, *Southern Honor: Ethics and Behavior in the Old South* (New York: Oxford University Press, 1982).

Index

Abel, 35
achievement as lessening shame, 12
Achilles, 102, 104, 106–7
Adam, 35, 50
Adler, Alfred, 18–19
Adorno, Theodor, 26
Aeneas, 81
Aeneid (Virgil), 37, 81
Aeschylus, 41
Agamemnon, 102, 104
Ajax, 104, 106
Albany, 77
Alcibiades, 111–13
All's Well That Ends Well, 123–4
ambition as stimulated by shame, 13, 46, 90–1
American South
  honor in, 76, 84
  as shame culture, 76
Amish, 36–7
Anabaptists, 33, 36–7
Ancient Greece
  guilt culture versus shame culture in, 34
  habitual behavior in, 10
  hubris, 34
  masculinity in, 75
  pride in, 34
Angelo
  Claudio and, 144
  honor and, 122
  Isabella and, 121–5, 127
  shame-ethics and, 122
  as stand-in for Vincentio, 120
Anna Karenina (Tolstoy), 80
anti-Semitism
  in England, 132–3
  in *The Merchant of Venice*, 131, 133
Antonio, 129–34
Antony and Cleopatra. See also specific character
  death in, 78, 81
  romantic love in, 78–80, 82
Apemantus, 109, 113

apocalyptic violence
  "apocalyptic fundamentalism," 114–15
  defined, 114
  in prisons, 113–14
  terrorism, 114–15
  in *Timon of Athens*, 108
Ariel, 129–30
Aristotle
  on ethics, 105
  on eyes, 7, 70
  on love, 28
  moral nihilism and, 98
  on need for love, 21
  on pride, 34
  on shame, 83
  on tragedy, 147
Augustine (Saint), 25, 35, 138
Augustus. *See* Octavius Caesar
Authoritarianism
  egalitarianism versus, 26
  moral nihilism and, 103
  rise of, 148

Bacon, Francis, 11
Banquo, 14, 90–1
Barbu, Zevedei, 33–4
Barnardine, 125
Barton, Anne, 101–2, 104
Bassiano, 133
Benedict, Ruth, 30–1, 34, 116–17
Bible
  The Acts of the Apostles, 33
  guilt culture versus shame culture in, 35
  guilt in, 99
  "Sermon on the Mount," 35, 57–8, 66, 97, 119
  violence in, 5
bin Laden, Osama, 13
Bloom, Harold, 79, 119–20, 131
Boas, Franz, 30–1, 116–17
Bolingbroke, 42, 46
Bonnie and Clyde, 76

As far as we know, humans are the only animals who create mirrors in which they can see and recognize themselves, not only as they appear to others, but also as to how they actually are (meaning "in reality," or "objectively"), thus advancing the Socratic recommendation to all humanity, *Gnothi Seauton*, or "Know Thyself." Plato, who extolled the importance of self-knowledge in many of his Dialogues (as have many other thinkers both during and since his time), saw this as the key to understanding human nature, thus enabling one to understand not only oneself but also others. Freud operationalized this advice by saying that the proper role of an analyst was to serve as a mirror to his or her patients, in whose reflection they could *see themselves* (meaning" *recognize*," or "*re-cognize*" themselves), in ways that they could not do as successfully without a mirror – which he saw as the key to overcoming, or healing from, psychopathology. Hamlet explicitly saw his "play within a play" as a way to hold up a mirror to his audience, that would enable them to recognize themselves, and for others to recognize them for who they actually were. What we are saying in this book is that on a much larger scale, Shakespeare, and his plays as a whole, hold up a mirror to all humanity, all society, to enable all of us to re-cognize – and hence understand – ourselves and each other, not only individually but also on a collective, political scale. And that developing the capacity to do just that may be the necessary key to prolonging the survival of our species. However relevant Shakespeare may have been at the turn of the seventeenth century, he has never been more relevant than he is now, at the beginning of the twenty-first.

Printed in Great Britain
by Amazon